ECONOMICS

IN
100 QUOTES

METRO BOOKS
New York

An Imprint of Sterling Publishing Co., Inc.
1166 Avenue of the Americas
New York, NY 10036

METRO BOOKS and the distinctive Metro Books logo are
registered trademarks of Sterling Publishing Co., Inc.

© 2018 Quarto Publishing plc

ISBN 978-1-4351-6778-0

For information about custom editions, special sales, and premium
and corporate purchases, please contact Sterling Special Sales
at 800-805-5489 or specialsales@sterlingpublishing.com.

Manufactured in Hong Kong

2 4 6 8 10 9 7 5 3 1

sterlingpublishing.com

Design by Tony Seddon

ECONOMICS

IN
100 QUOTES

DAN
SMITH

METRO BOOKS
New York

INTRODUCTION

Economics can seem a dry and dusty subject, concerned with little more than how you can make money or how you cope when you don't have enough of the stuff. Appearances can be deceptive, though. Economics is about much more than just money. Economics is actually all about *us*—how we as human beings manage our limited resources against our unlimited needs and desires. Writing in the Victorian age, British economist Alfred Marshall defined the field as nothing more and nothing less than "a study of mankind in the ordinary business of life."

Yet economics has had a bad rap over the years. Thomas Carlyle, the noted historian and essayist, condemned it as the "dismal science"—a tag that has stubbornly stuck. Among its features that he found so unpalatable was the idea that we might find "the secret of this Universe in 'supply and demand.'" It is true that economics can sometimes seem unappealingly reductionist, taking complex, highly charged human conditions and analyzing them through the lens of cool, unemotional concepts. However, economics is actually an incredibly vibrant field.

Certain economic concepts may seem emotionless, but they are usually employed in a bid to impose some degree of rational order on some of the most disordered aspects of our existence. Moreover, modern economics has long embraced the idea that psychology, emotion, and downright irrationality are important considerations when attempting any serious economic modeling. Strip away the mind-bending numbers and complex equations and you will find a subject whose real interest is in human interaction. How do we share out nature's bounty? How do we use it to produce the things people really want and need? How do we make sure everyone has enough to get on with? How do we create a world that is fair and one that looks after its resources with an eye to the future?

The hundred quotations that follow cannot, of course, tell the whole story of economics. What they aim to do instead is to give a broad overview of the subject. Included are the words of great philosophers of the ancient world as they struggled with such basic questions as how far we should seek to satisfy our wants, as well as whether the natural world should be held in common ownership or dispersed among private individuals. Then there are the voices of some of the founding fathers of the modern economic discipline—great Enlightenment figures like Adam Smith and David Ricardo—along with those whose economic ideologies actively shaped vast swathes of the world—from Karl Marx in the 19th century to John Maynard Keynes and Milton Friedman.

Moving on to the modern day, we have the thoughts of some of our sharpest contemporary economists as they wrestle with the Great Recession that took the world by surprise in the first decade of this century, struggle to address issues of rising inequality, and lay down routes to an equitable and sustainable future. As well as trained economists, there are also the views of assorted politicians, authors, historians, cultural commentators, and religious figures—each of them bringing something of value to the table. A good many of the quotations are controversial, while others reflect particular historical attitudes. Their inclusion in these pages is not a reflection of how "true" or "correct" they are—rather, they serve to shed light on the development of economic thinking and illustrate just how contentious the field can be.

As Keynes put it: "The ideas of economists and political philosophers, both when they are right and when they are wrong, are more powerful than is commonly understood. Indeed, the world is ruled by little else." The quotations contained herein give a flavor of why this is the case. They may even offer some kernel of hope that we might eventually get things right.

There is no calamity greater than lavish desires. There is no greater guilt than discontentment. And there is no greater disaster than greed.

01

LAOZI
ca. 6th century BCE (ASSUMED)

SOURCE: *Dao De Jing*
DATE: ca. 6th century BCE
FIELD: Demand

Laozi, a close contemporary of Confucius, is widely credited with being the author of the *Dao De Jing*, the founding document of Daoism (although its authorship is a subject of enduring academic debate). He is a figure of immense importance in Chinese philosophy and has contributed to molding long periods of Chinese political thought.

Laozi believed that by entertaining lavish desires, individuals and societies as a whole put themselves on the road to ruin. He acknowledged that we each have needs that must be fulfilled, and recognized that desire can be a positive force. However, he warned against the blind hunger for "more" in a material sense. As he framed it, "To have enough of enough is always enough." Moreover, by overcoming our naked desires, we give ourselves the best chance of reaching our full potential. "Be frugal," he wrote, "and you can be liberal; avoid putting yourself before others and you can become a leader among men."

His emphasis on the nobility of frugality—that the curtailing of desire opens the way to happiness—is echoed throughout Eastern philosophy, from the teachings of the Buddha (see page 9) to those of Hinduism, and continues to appeal to large numbers of people throughout the world. It is a view that informs Chinese society today. The belief that collective effort may provide enough for everyone has underpinned the Communist ideology that has prevailed since the mid-20th century, even if its practical results have been notoriously mixed—the devastating famine that accompanied the drive for agricultural collectivization in the 1950s and 1960s representing a particularly negative outcome.

Craving and desire
are the cause of all
unhappiness.

02

SIDDHARTHA GAUTAMA

ca. 563–483 BCE

SOURCE: Tripitaka
DATE: ca. 533 BCE
FIELD: Asceticism

Siddhartha Gautama is better known to the world as the Buddha ("the one who is enlightened"). His enlightenment may be said to have evolved from his shock at realizing the extent of economic inequality in the world. Born into a powerful and privileged family in Lumbini, in what is now Nepal, it is related that his father guarded him from the grim realities of life that most ordinary people faced. However, during his twenties the inquisitive Gautama became appalled by the deprivations he witnessed others suffering as a result of ill-health, old age, and poverty.

He began to develop his philosophy that suffering resulted from unsatisfied want and desire, and that the fulfillment of one's sensual desires (for food, wealth, physical love, and so on) brings only fleeting satisfaction. Gautama took up the life of an ascetic, living by a code of strict self-discipline and abstention from indulgence, begging for alms and practicing meditation. However, when this lifestyle almost resulted in his death from starvation, he began to champion a "Middle Way" between the sensual life and asceticism.

Referring to our desires and wants as "attachments," he suggested that the root cause of human suffering and dissatisfaction will be removed if we free ourselves from our attachments. In order to do this, he suggested, we must become unyoked from the self (that is to say, the desires of the self). With some half a billion adherents in the world today, Buddhism remains a highly influential set of doctrines, not least in its radical reassessment of traditional economic assumptions.

IT IS CLEARLY BETTER THAT
PROPERTY SHOULD BE **PRIVATE**.

03

ARISTOTLE

384–322 BCE

SOURCE: *Politics*
DATE: ca. mid-4th century BCE
FIELD: Property

Aristotle strongly advocated the private ownership of property, in contrast to the common ownership championed by Plato. According to Aristotle, "When everyone has a distinct interest, men will make more progress because everyone will be attending to his own business." It was a view that would be adopted by some of the leading figures of modern economic theory, not least Adam Smith (see page 29) in the 18th century.

Aristotle contended that selfishness is ingrained in the human character and cannot be legislated out by such artifices as common ownership. Indeed, to attempt to eliminate the trait, he suggested, is to deny the individual the opportunity of full self-expression and self-realization. Moreover, since private property is necessary for exercising virtues such as generosity and hospitality, it is integral to the pursuit of a virtuous life, which Aristotle considered the ultimate good. Furthermore, private property gives its owner a sense of happiness—a virtue in itself—and fosters personal and civic responsibility.

Where Plato argued for common ownership of property and its produce, Aristotle said that resentment would fester between those who work hard and yet receive the same as those who work less. For Aristotle, the best social model has land privately owned but its produce available for common use. Individuals may thus aspire to private property themselves while reaping the benefits of toiling on another's property (say, as a tenant farmer). The contrasting positions of Aristotle and Plato can be regarded as an early instance of the ongoing ideological battle between socialism and capitalism.

ECONOMY IS TOO LATE WHEN THE

BOTTOM HAS BEEN REACHED.

04

ca. 4 BCE–65 CE

SOURCE: *Epistulae Morales ad Lucilium (The Moral Epistles)*
DATE: ca. 65 CE
FIELD: Prudence

Raised in Rome, Seneca became a tutor and advisor to the emperor, Nero, before he was forced to take his own life for allegedly plotting to assassinate the emperor (although his involvement is far from certain). In his extraordinary life, Seneca acquired vast riches and lived a most comfortable existence. However, as—like Epictetus—an avowed Stoic, he worried immensely about how the individual ought to navigate their relationship with material wealth.

His observation in the quote opposite comes from a series of letters (perhaps written as fiction) to the putative procurator of Sicily, which aimed to provide moral guidance across a range of subjects. It references an earlier quote by the Greek poet Hesiod: "Take your fill when the cask is first opened and when it is nearly spent, but midways be sparing: it is poor saving when you come to the end." In other words, use your wealth sensibly when it is plentiful and so avoid the threat of it running out altogether.

While his personal riches made it difficult for Seneca to argue that the individual should rein in his desires completely, he nonetheless believed that we should strive to ensure we do not become slaves to material wants. "We would belong to ourselves if those things were not ours," he once said, suggesting that material desires represent a disease rather than "a thirst." Though he has faced accusations of hypocrisy over the centuries, given his own affluent lifestyle, his letters nonetheless outline a prudent approach to economic management that has retained its appeal across the generations.

Love of money
is the root of all evil.

05

ASCRIBED TO THE APOSTLE PAUL
ca. 5–CA. 67

SOURCE: First Epistle of Paul to Timothy
DATE: ca. 1st century CE
FIELD: Avarice

Encapsulating the New Testament's attitude to wealth, Paul's words have had enduring influence across the world—even if their sentiment has not always been adhered to by those who consider themselves godly. In one of the most misquoted quotations of all time, Paul did not suggest money itself is the root of all evil, but rather our *love* of money. It is a vital distinction.

In assorted biblical passages, money is recognized as a useful tool for doing good. In Proverbs, for instance, showing generosity to the needy is cited as a way of honoring God. Moreover, wealth is no obstacle to being considered godly, as in the case of Job, whose godliness was rewarded by having his material losses compensated twofold. But the Bible does warn against considering material wealth to be a virtue in itself. Proverbs, for example, states that "He who trusts in his riches will fall, but the righteous shall flourish as the green leaf."

It is Paul's quotation, though—with its argument that desire for material wealth is injurious to spiritual well-being—that has perhaps most closely informed the approach to wealth in Christian societies for some two millennia. It was, for instance, one of the key arguments used by Martin Luther when attacking the financially acquisitive Roman Catholic Church of the Middle Ages. Still today, it offers a challenging alternative to the "greed is good" culture that predominates in many corners of the globe's capitalist societies.

Wealth consists not in having great possessions, but in having few wants.

06

EPICTETUS

ca. 55–135 CE

SOURCE: Recorded in *The Discourses*, compiled by his pupil Arrian, ca. 108 CE.
DATE: ca. 108 CE
FIELD: Demand

Born as a slave in what is now Turkey, Epictetus was given his freedom by his owner. It is tempting to think that his lowly origins influenced his belief that wealth does not directly correlate to the extent of one's possessions. Rather, richness ought to be measured by the extent to which one's desires are satisfied. This ties in with the modern idea that economics is less about acquisition *per se*, than how limited resources may best be directed to meet our wants and needs.

Central to his philosophy is the idea that certain aspects of the world are within the individual's control while others are not. We may thus control "whatever are our own actions" (which, he said, includes pursuit, desire, and aversion), while we must cede control of "whatever are not our own actions" (among them, property). By taking command of (and limiting) our desires, we ensure that what we can attain is sufficient to satisfy our wants—arguably a perfect realization of the economist's dream.

His views were rooted in Stoic philosophy. Stoicism suggests that happiness is to be found by dispassionately accepting whatever happens (since external events are beyond our control), while insisting that the individual takes responsibility for their own actions. Instead of endlessly pursuing the fulfillment of our desires (as is the accepted aim of modern capitalist societies), he argued instead for his alternative approach since "If we wish for nothing but what God wills, we shall be truly free."

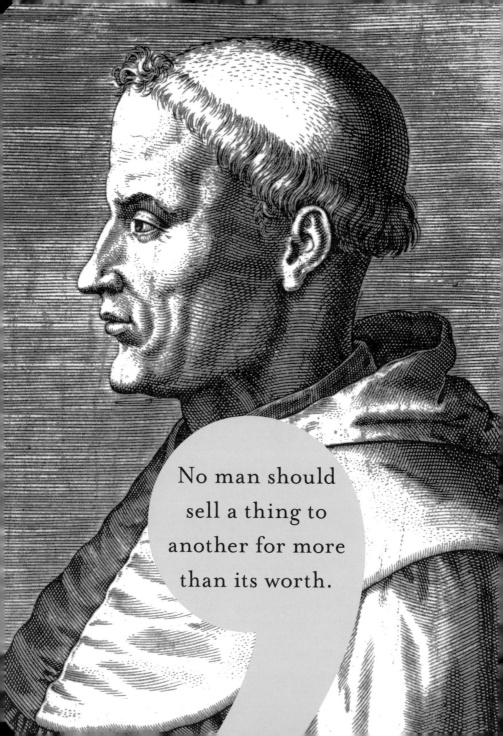

No man should sell a thing to another for more than its worth.

07

THOMAS AQUINAS
1225–1274

SOURCE: *Summa Theologica*
DATE: 1274
FIELD: Trade

A Dominican monk, Thomas Aquinas wrote *Summa Theologica* as an instructional guide for theology students to illustrate that philosophical reason follows on from Christian belief. In regard to economics, he sought to show that fair dealing in trade is a moral imperative, while encouraging a reassessment of the civil laws that governed commerce.

Central to his argument is the notion that "To sell something more dearly than it is worth, or buy it more cheaply, in itself is unjust and illicit." This ran contrary to the widely held (and often legally enshrined) position that a trader may rightfully buy cheap and sell expensively. While Aquinas acknowledged that human law necessarily allows much that divine law rejects, he nonetheless argued that civil law should demand compensation, if a seller charges a price excessively above what might be considered the just price (although exactly what constituted a just price remained open to debate).

Aquinas also rejected the view that the desire to buy low and sell high was a natural instinct, instead considering it a vice. "Buying and selling seem to be established for the common advantage of both parties," he said, "one of whom requires that which belongs to the other, and vice versa [...] Now whatever is established for the common advantage, should not be more of a burden to one party than to another." Therefore, he contended, by buying an item for less than its worth, or selling it for more, "there is no longer the equality of justice" and so the trade is in itself unjust and unlawful.

The price of any commodity

rises or **falls**

by the proportion of the
number of buyers and sellers.

08

JOHN LOCKE

1632–1704

SOURCE: *Some Considerations on the Consequences of the Lowering of Interest and the Raising of the Value of Money*
DATE: 1691
FIELD: Supply and demand

John Locke was one of the Enlightenment's greatest thinkers and is widely considered the father of modern liberalism. He also held several prominent official positions, including Secretary of the Board of Trade, which molded much of his thought on questions of economics.

His investigations into the theory of supply and demand—that is to say, the factors affecting the supply and demand of goods and services in the market and the relationship between them—were especially notable. Though he was not the coiner of the phrase "supply and demand" (James Denham-Steuart used it in his 1767 work, *Inquiry into the Principles of Political Economy*, and Adam Smith explored the notion in *The Wealth of Nations* in 1776), Locke's framing of the concept in *Some Considerations* was remarkable for its clarity and precision.

In the quotation cited opposite, he identifies that market price is determined by the level of demand for a product in relation to the volume of it that is available. In simple terms, if two people want something and there is only one such item available, the price will go up. But where two suppliers are competing for a single buyer, the price will go down. As Locke put it, "That which regulates the price [of goods] is nothing else but their quantity in proportion to their rent [i.e. the level of demand]." In the early years of the 19th century, Antoine Augustin Cournot would notably build upon Locke's work as he constructed a mathematical model of the phenomenon.

When the riches are engrossed by a few, these must contribute very largely to the supplying of the public necessities.

09

DAVID HUME

1711–1776

SOURCE: *Of Commerce*
DATE: 1752
FIELD: Taxation

Although David Hume is perhaps best known for his examination of human nature and lacked the overarching economic vision of his close contemporary Adam Smith, he was nonetheless an important figure in the development of modern economic thought. For instance, Nobel laureate Paul Krugman has said in relation to Hume's *Of the Balance of Trade* (published in 1752), "David Hume created what I consider the first true economic model."

His views on private property were nuanced. While rejecting it as a natural right, he accepted it as justifiable within society, where resources are limited. Contending that "It is well known that men's happiness consists not so much in an abundance of [commodities], as in the peace and security with which they possess them," he believed that, were property to be distributed equally among all citizens, there would be no motivation to practice thrift or hard work. Regarding perfect equality as the fast track to impoverishment for society as a whole, he therefore preferred the concept of private property.

Yet as his quotation opposite reveals, though he thought some degree of economic inequality was desirable, too much leads to a weakening of society as the poor become incapable of resisting the rich. As power devolves ever more to the rich and the poor are further impoverished, industry and innovation are stifled and society as a whole suffers. Therefore, he demanded, the rich should shoulder the greater responsibility for supplying certain public necessities—a model of progressive taxation of the type widely implemented throughout the world today.

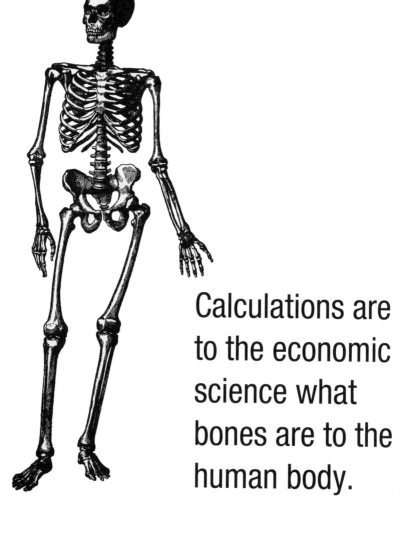

Calculations are to the economic science what bones are to the human body.

10

FRANÇOIS QUESNAY
1694–1774

SOURCE: Letter to the Marquis of Mirabeau
DATE: ca. 1758
FIELD: Economic science

François Quesnay, for a while physician to King Louis XV, was a leading member of the physiocratic school of economics, which believed that nations derive their wealth solely from the value of the produce of their land. It also contended that government should hold back from interfering with natural economic law. Though much of the detail of the physiocratic worldview has been disproven over time, it nonetheless represents one of the earliest fully formed theories of macroeconomics—and Quesnay was vital in bringing scientific rigor and analysis to the study of economics. He expanded on the quotation opposite by saying, "Without them [calculations] it will always be a vague and confused science, at the mercy of error and prejudice."

Quesnay's single greatest contribution was his 1758 *Tableau économique* (*Economic Table*), which became in effect the manifesto of the physiocrats. Using mathematical formulae, Quesnay sought to show how agricultural products (the sole source of national wealth, according to his theory) ought to be distributed among the landowning class, the agricultural workers, manufacturers, and merchants, so as to increase the overall production of the state (and thus increase its wealth). Complex, demanding, and at times highly abstract, it was nonetheless a remarkable feat of analysis that put cool, unemotional mathematics at its heart—and signposted the way to the future of economic study. In the estimation of the Marquis of Mirabeau, Quesnay's *Table* was nothing less than one of the three principle inventions that contributed to social stability—along with writing and money.

Small debts are like small shot
[...] rattling on every side,
and can scarcely be escaped
without a wound;

great debts are like cannon:
of loud noise, but little danger.

11

SAMUEL JOHNSON
1709–1784

SOURCE: Letter to Joseph Simpson
DATE: ca. 1759
FIELD: Debt

In this advice to a friend, Samuel Johnson tapped into fundamental truths about the nature of debt. Indeed, John Maynard Keynes was to make a similar point in the mid-20th century with his observation: "If you owe your bank a hundred pounds, you have a problem, but if you owe it a million, it has." The global financial collapse that began in 2008 brought renewed relevance to the question of personal indebtedness.

Johnson's point is that relatively low-level debt puts chronic strain on the debtor, who bears the burden almost exclusively. The creditor (assuming they have a reasonable level of financial security themselves) may rightfully pursue the debt, and feel the benefit of extra interest accruing as it goes unpaid, without fear of economic capitulation in their own right. By contrast, a larger debt imposes a greater level of pressure on the creditor, since they will likely have stretched themselves to offer the loan in the first place. Under these circumstances, it is in the interests of the creditor to "nurse" the debtor through until the debt can be repaid.

Imagine, for example, a stallholder with stock worth a hundred dollars and a debt of the same value. The creditor may take the stock in repayment, and destroy the stallholder's business. But if he owes a thousand dollars, it is more advantageous for the creditor to assist him in growing his business so that the larger debt may be paid off in the future. The great debt thus may make much more noise than the smaller but be far less dangerous to the debtor.

Wherever there is great property, there is great inequality.

12

ADAM SMITH
1723–1790

SOURCE: *The Wealth of Nations*
DATE: 1776
FIELD: Economic equality

The Wealth of Nations is widely regarded as the founding text of modern economics. Looking at economic functioning in the age of the Industrial Revolution, Adam Smith gave a wide-ranging analysis that took in labor, productivity, and the markets. Perhaps most notably, he introduced the concept of the "invisible hand" (looked at more fully on page 131). But his ideas on economic inequality were also highly innovative.

While at first sight the quotation opposite might suggest Smith was warning against the dangers of private property and the injustices of inequality, his position is rather more complex. He fundamentally believed that markets should largely be left to their own devices and recommended only very limited government intervention to provide those social goods and services that he believed the market would otherwise fail to adequately furnish. Indeed, he regarded a level of economic inequality as evidence of a well-functioning commercial society. His observation, "For one very rich man, there must be at least five hundred poor, and the affluence of the few presupposes the indigence of the many," was really a call to arms, warning that the modern market economy must have strong institutions of civil law or else face deep civil discord.

However, Smith's words also represented a new approach to poverty. Specifically, he treats poverty not as an absolute concept (as had traditionally been the case) but as a relative state. As such, he began the long and continuing journey into the causes and impacts of economic inequality (namely, relative levels of wealth), setting aside fixed notions of what constitutes rich and poor.

In this world nothing can be said to be certain, except death and taxes.

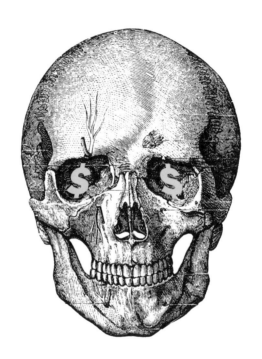

13

BENJAMIN FRANKLIN

1706-1790

SOURCE: Letter to Jean-Baptiste Leroy
DATE: 1789
FIELD: Taxation

Benjamin Franklin was an extraordinary polymath—scientist, philosopher, publisher, entrepreneur, politician, not to mention one of the Founding Fathers of the United States. In fact, it was in reference to the recently enacted US Constitution that Franklin was referring when he made his famous quote: "Our new Constitution is now established, and has an appearance that promises permanency; but in this world nothing can be said to be certain, except death and taxes." Furthermore, he was paraphrasing an observation made by Christopher Bullock in his 1716 work, *The Cobbler of Preston*: "'Tis impossible to be sure of anything but Death and Taxes."

Of course, though death is inevitable, taxation is not, but Franklin was nonetheless making a pertinent point—tax was (and remains) very difficult to escape. And in America, it was a particularly prickly issue at the time. For much of their early post-Columbian history, the North American territories had been largely tax-free. It was simmering resentment at the perceived unfairness of the levels of tax demanded of settlers by their colonial overlords in London that brought about the American Revolutionary War.

There are today a handful of tax-free or low-tax territories around the world, most of them very small, but in much of the developed world, citizens can expect an individual tax burden equivalent to anywhere between 30 percent and 60 percent of their income. The debate rages among economists as to whether societies function best by the redistribution of wealth that taxation permits or whether lower taxes promote broadly healthier economies. Meanwhile, Franklin's words remain a truism.

Give me control of a nation's money supply, and I care not who makes its laws.

MAYER AMSCHEL ROTHSCHILD

MAYER AMSCHEL ROTHSCHILD

1744–1812

SOURCE: Cited in a letter from economist T. C. Daniel to US president Woodrow Wilson in 1913
DATE: ca. 1790
FIELD: Monetary policy

Mayer Amschel Rothschild is one of the giants in the history of banking, the founder of the Rothschild dynasty and an original master of international finance. Whether or not he said the words opposite is a source of some contention, yet the matter is almost academic. Regardless of their origin, they encapsulate a certain view of international banking in particular and economics as a whole.

Underpinning their sense is the idea that real power lies not with a monarch or emperor, or even a democratically elected parliament, but with those who hold the purse strings. Since as early as the 12th century, the Knights Templar had shown how a small organization could gain huge influence by developing a nascent form of modern banking. Rothschild, though, took banking on several stages, earning the trust of many in Europe's ruling class and using the circumstances of international conflict (during which time demand for credit from warring parties increases) to consolidate his bank's wealth and influence.

Rothschild realized that in an age when belief in the divine right of kings was waning, banks held the whip hand. The stability of countries relied less on the strength of their leaders than their ability to ensure sufficient money in the economy that people might be furnished with enough to keep them happy, or at least supplicant. Even today, governments operate monetary policy on much the same principle. Moreover, the global financial upheavals of the early part of this century revealed the extent to which nations remain subject to the actions of their bankers.

If we command our wealth, we shall be rich and free; if our wealth commands us, we are poor indeed.

6

EDMUND BURKE

1730-1797

SOURCE: *Letters on a Regicide Peace*
DATE: 1796
FIELD: Wealth

Despite being a long-serving member of the British parliament for the Whig Party (the forerunner of the Liberal Party), Edmund Burke is now widely considered the forefather of modern conservatism. In 1790 he wrote *Reflections on the Revolution in France*, an impassioned critique of the French Revolution. Appalled by the violence being unleashed on continental Europe, he argued instead for gradual reform as far preferable to bloody uprising. Predictably, then, he was a fierce opponent of moves by the British government of William Pitt to reach a peace with the revolutionary French Directorate. He put down his objections in four letters, which were published as *Letters on a Regicide Peace*, from which the quotation opposite is taken.

His words were intended to serve as a warning to the British government against letting economic considerations unduly mold its broader policies. Burke was convinced that concern for not upsetting Britain's relative economic stability was pushing Westminster toward a huge foreign policy error. In simplistic terms, he believed that the job of the economy is to serve as a tool, to facilitate good things. But should the economy, in all its abstraction, become the "boss" (whether of government, other bodies, or the individual), it is likely to result in incorrect action. Believing Pitt's government was being driven by the desire to preserve national wealth, Burke wrote: "We are bought by the enemy with the treasure from our own coffers." "Often has a man lost his all," he continued, "because he would not submit to hazard all in defending it."

To prevent the recurrence of misery is, alas! beyond the power of man.

16

THOMAS MALTHUS

1766–1834

SOURCE: *Essay on the Principle of Population*
DATE: 1798
FIELD: Sustainability

Thomas Malthus was an English clergyman and political economist who originated the so-called "Malthusian Problem," summed up in the rather depressing quotation opposite. Central to the Malthusian problem is the assertion that "The power of population is indefinitely greater than the power in the earth to produce subsistence for man." Malthus believed that population levels remain fairly constant over the long run as a result of the planet's inability to support significant increases for more than short periods. With finite land on which to grow food (and with productivity only marginally affected by increasing labor inputs), Malthus argued that rising populations will always bring about food shortages. This in turn prompts a rise in the death rate and a fall in the birth rate (since parents cannot afford to feed another mouth), until population numbers level out and the cycle begins again.
In basic economic terms, he contended that economic stagnation will always rein in population growth. Hence, "To prevent the recurrence of misery is, alas! beyond the power of man."

Malthus's assumptions flew in the face of Enlightenment orthodoxy that human progress was inexorable. Moreover, his ideas lost traction over time as the advance of technology (not least in agricultural production) resulted in more than two centuries of rapid global population expansion. Nonetheless, such eminent figures as John Maynard Keynes remained intrigued by his arguments. Today, there is renewed interest in what he had to say, not least among those—economists and laymen alike—who fear our planet is reaching its capacity, leading to ferocious competition in some regions for resources as basic as water.

A product is no sooner created, than it, from that instant, affords a market for other products to the full extent of its own value.

JEAN BAPTISTE SAY
1767–1832

SOURCE: *A Treatise on Political Economy*
DATE: 1803
FIELD: Supply and demand

An economist and businessman, Jean-Baptiste Say's words (characterized as Say's Law) seek to explain the nature of markets. The quotation continues: "When the producer has put the finishing hand to his product, he is most anxious to sell it immediately, lest its value should diminish in his hands. Nor is he less anxious to dispose of the money he may get for it; for the value of money is also perishable. But the only way of getting rid of money is in the purchase of some product or other. Thus the mere circumstance of creation of one product immediately opens a vent for other products."

Say's arguments suggest that economies ought to be permanently close to full employment, since there will be no job losses resulting from collapsing demand. Furthermore, economic downturns cannot be the result of overproduction, since production creates demand. Therefore, in order to boost overall output, economists should look at increasing production, while letting demand look after itself.

It has subsequently been shown that Say made a number of inaccurate assumptions. The global downturn of the 1930s, for example, proved that it is possible to produce at a rate that outstrips demand, precipitating a downward economic cycle. In addition, people do stockpile money—either as part of a planned savings regime or because wider economic circumstances render them nervous to part with their cash. Nonetheless, his ideas predominated for large parts of the 19th century and remain a powerful source of debate today too, as economists struggle to discern whether economies are boosted most by increasing demand or supply.

A large income
is the best recipe
for happiness I
ever heard of.

18

JANE AUSTEN
1775–1817

SOURCE: *Mansfield Park*
DATE: 1814
FIELD: Feminist economics

Jane Austen is famed for six novels, each a comical and incisive critique of late 18th- and early 19th-century life. Among her most important contributions to the documenting of the social fabric is her rendering of the economic plight of women, not only in Britain in this specific period but around the world and spanning much of human history. Austen brought to mainstream attention the challenges faced by generations of single women whose financial security rested almost entirely upon their making a "good" marriage (that is to say, to a man of wealth or, at the very least, good prospects).

In *Mansfield Park*, Mary Crawford (the character who utters the words quoted opposite) is torn between her desire to marry one Thomas Bertram, the heir of a baronet, and her emotional attachment to his younger brother, Edmund, whose financial future is much less certain, especially as he intends to take religious orders. As she informs him: "Be honest and poor, by all means— but I shall not envy you; I do not much think I shall even respect you. I have a much greater respect for those that are honest and rich."

Over the subsequent centuries there has been significant progress in terms of the opportunities open to women across much of the developed world to achieve economic independence. Nonetheless, many of the problems that Austen conjured with remain a challenge to swathes of the global female population—from young girls urged into arranged marriages for economic reasons to women confronted by "glass ceilings" and unequal pay in the workplace.

A country may, in return for manufactured commodities, import corn, even if it can be grown with less labor than in the country from which it is imported.

DAVID RICARDO
1772–1823

SOURCE: *On the Principles of Political Economy and Taxation*
DATE: 1817
FIELD: Comparative advantage

A leading figure in classical economics, among David Ricardo's many achievements was his explication of the idea of comparative advantage in international trade. Adam Smith had championed the idea of free trade as beneficial to all, based on principles of absolute advantage, whereby a country exports those goods and services that it can produce more efficiently than its competitors.

There was a problem, though: Where a county has no absolute advantage, it risks losing out on trade altogether. Ricardo explained, however, that trade could be mutually beneficial even where one nation dominates in terms of absolute advantage. The trick, he suggested, was for the dominant country to concentrate on exports in which its absolute advantage is greater, and import where the advantage was lesser. Hence his suggestion about importing corn from a country even where it takes greater effort to grow it.

Say it takes 5 man-hours for Country A to produce a pound of corn, and for Country B, 8 hours. To produce a gallon of beer, A takes 6 hours and B, 7 hours. In other words, it takes A 11 hours to produce a pound of corn and a gallon of beer, while it takes B 15 hours. Altogether, that is 26 hours for 2 pounds of corn and 2 gallons of beer. By specializing, A could produce 2.2 pounds of corn in its 11 hours, and B 2.14 gallons of beer in its 15 hours. Thus overall, production is higher as a result of specialization, and each country can benefit from trading its excess.

Universal competition or the effort to always produce more, and always at a lower price [...] has been a dangerous system.

20

1773–1842

SOURCE: *Nouveaux Principes d'économie politique*
(New Principles of Political Economy)
DATE: 1819
FIELD: Competition

Jean-Charles Sismondi took on several of the economic orthodoxies of his age, driven by a belief that economists ought to be less focused on how to spur growth and more interested in how wealth may be used to increase happiness. "Increased wealth is not the goal of political economy," he noted, "but the means it has to procure happiness for everyone." He is today probably most famous for his study of how unregulated competition contributes to increasing inequality between those who have property and those who don't.

Looking at post-Industrial Revolution England, where the economy was booming amid a free-market free-for-all, Sismondi saw much to disturb him. Where some marveled at the vast accumulation of wealth by a growing class of entrepreneurs and risk-takers, Sismondi saw a corresponding spike in those facing poverty. Farmers and craftsmen who were until recently able to make a reasonable living for themselves and their families now had little more status than unskilled wage-workers.

The rapid expansion of technology might have been to the great advantage of factory owners and merchants, but many ordinary workers found they were no longer needed. Moreover, the desire to bring more of everything to market with ever greater speed and efficiency (and all at a lower price) led to economic peaks and troughs that disrupted the social fabric and left many facing ruin. If this is the free-market dream, Sismondi suggested, we should be very wary. Although not a socialist himself, his teachings were nevertheless influential on a new generation of thinkers that included Karl Marx and Friedrich Engels.

The theory of the Communists may be summed up in the single sentence: **Abolition of Private Property.**

21

KARL MARX / FRIEDRICH ENGELS
1818-1883 / 1820-1895

SOURCE: *The Communist Manifesto*
DATE: 1848
FIELD: Communism

Written as socialism—the idea that the means of production, distribution, and exchange should be owned and/or regulated by the community as a whole—was gaining increasing support in Europe, *The Communist Manifesto* was a landmark work of political economy. In it, the authors expounded their radical vision of a communist idyll.

Marx and Engels believed that mankind's destiny is determined by political and economic factors played out through history. Human history is, the *Manifesto* said, "the history of class struggles." It traced a path from an ancient system of common ownership, through one rooted in private property and slavery, on to feudalism and then capitalism. Each was characterized, the theory went, by one social group dominating another. In the age of capitalism, a minority class of property owners (the bourgeoisie) benefited by exploiting the mass of wage-laborers (the proletariat). But as wealth becomes ever more concentrated, Marx and Engels contended, the number of the discontented proletariat will increase until they overthrow the bourgeoisie in revolutions. Capitalism will be succeeded by a system of perfect common ownership—in other words, the end of private property. "Let the ruling classes tremble at a Communistic revolution. The proletarians have nothing to lose but their chains," concluded the *Manifesto*. "They have a world to win."

Although it was not until 1917 that Russia became the first communist state—long after Marx and Engels had died—their ideas of economic reorganization would influence the lives of millions, for better and worse, in the 20th century and beyond.

Capitalists can do nothing without laborers, nor the laborers without capital.

22

JOHN STUART MILL

JOHN STUART MILL
1806–1873

SOURCE: *Principles of Political Economy*
DATE: 1848
FIELD: Economic systems

As a utilitarian, Mill believed in individual liberty in pursuit of the greatest happiness for the greatest number. He was by inclination suspicious of excessive intervention by the state or indeed any other social group. This was reflected in his dissatisfaction with both the capitalist and socialist models that dominated European thought in his lifetime. Instead he investigated the possibility of a hybrid system in which every individual has the ability to develop their full potential.

Mill was by no means blind to certain of the advantages inherent in both capitalism and socialism. He was a defender, for example, of aspects of free-market competition but disliked the damage unfettered capitalism wrought on individuals and whole communities. He also recognized the unfairness of those with inherited wealth having "an advantage which they may have in no way deserved."

Nonetheless, he saw the relationship between the property-owning class and the property-less workers as ultimately mutually beneficial. Laborers, he suggested, share in the advantage of inherited wealth, though not to an equal extent as the inheritors. This was because the capitalist (property owner) can produce nothing without the efforts of the laborer, but nor can the laborer work and earn without capital input. Moreover, just as workers compete for employment, so do capitalists compete for labor, so allowing for the circulation of capital around the economy. It may be an imperfect system, Mill suggested, but it is by uniting the interests of the capitalist and the worker that economic progression becomes possible.

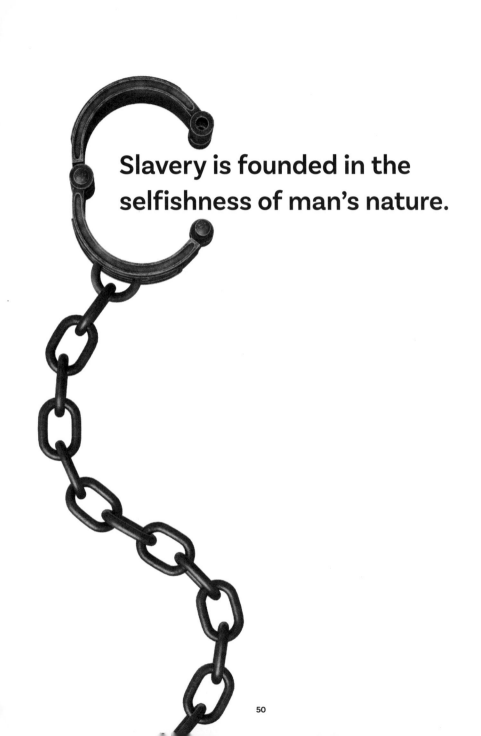

Slavery is founded in the selfishness of man's nature.

23

ABRAHAM LINCOLN
1809–1865

SOURCE: Peoria speech
DATE: 1854
FIELD: Slavery

Slavery has, of course, been practiced since ancient times, but by the 19th century there was growing unease about it in post-Enlightenment societies. All the great European imperial powers, as well as the territories of North America, had grown rich by exploiting slave labor. While there were few attempts to justify the practice morally (ideas of blacks being "lesser" than whites stubbornly persisted), there were grave concerns among those who had reaped the benefits of slavery that their wealth might dissipate with its abolition.

This was no more evident than in the southern states of the USA. Indeed in 1854, the US Congress passed the Kansas-Nebraska Act that threatened to actively expand slavery throughout the American Midwest. For Abraham Lincoln, future American president, the question was not whether the US could afford to do away with slavery, but whether it could afford not to. Despite the immediate economic consequences, he was convinced that slavery must end in order for the country to move forward. Not only did he say that slavery is founded in man's selfishness but that "opposition to it, [is rooted] in his love of justice."

In bare economic terms, Lincoln argued that slaves had the same right to rise in life and to enjoy the fruits of their labor as anyone else. By freedom, he would later say, "the weak … grow stronger, the ignorant, wiser; and all better, and happier together." Slavery would end in the US under Lincoln's presidency in 1863, by which time an estimated 12.5 million Africans had been shipped to the New World.

Wealth is not possession but enjoyment.

HENRY DAVID THOREAU

1817–1862

SOURCE: Letter to Harrison Gray Otis Blake
DATE: 1856
FIELD: Materialism

The idea of "going back to basics" and living closer to nature was one that long fascinated Henry David Thoreau. As a transcendentalist, he was wary of the impact that institutions have upon the individual, instead arguing that every person should live independently and self-reliantly. It was a belief he put into action when he spent more than two years living in a rudimentary cabin amid Massachusetts woodland owned by his great mentor, Ralph Waldo Emerson.

While thoroughly removed from the heated debates between advocates of the capitalist and socialist systems that largely dominated 19th- and 20th-century economic discourse, Thoreau's ideas nonetheless found a significant and receptive audience. Indeed, his admonition to be content with what one has (he identified only four necessities: food, shelter, clothing, and fuel) echoes the earlier teachings of many of the great Eastern philosophers. "I am grateful for what I am & have," he wrote. "My thanksgiving is perpetual. It is surprising how contented one can be with nothing definite—only a sense of existence [...] O how I laugh when I think of my vague indefinite riches. No run on my bank can drain it—for my wealth is not possession but enjoyment."

While his ideas never gained a foothold in the mainstream, his teachings have nonetheless endured. We may draw a direct line between the anti-materialism of Thoreau and any number of "alternative lifestyle" advocates that we have today, many arguing that going "off grid" and reducing our reliance on an increasingly globalized economic system represents the true road to happiness.

I have attempted to
treat Economy as a Calculus
of Pleasure and Pain.

STANLEY JEVONS

1835–1882

SOURCE: *The Theory of Political Economy*
DATE: 1871
FIELD: Utility

Stanley Jevons was among the earliest generations of economists who attempted to systematically impose mathematics on the field of economic analysis. His *Theory of Political Economy* represented the most full explication of his ideas, and it is in its introduction that the words opposite can be found.

In describing his "Calculus of Pleasure and Pain," he was touching upon the subject of utility—that is to say, the amount of satisfaction or pleasure that is derived from consuming a particular good or service. Utility is considered a driving force of consumer behavior, since individuals are assumed to make purchasing decisions on the basis of what will make them most happy under a given set of circumstances.

The idea of utility entered into mainstream academic discourse with the emergence of utilitarianism as a philosophy in the 19th century (championed by Jeremy Bentham and John Stuart Mill), and its emphasis on pain and pleasure. Yet defining and measuring such concepts was, and remains, highly problematic. Nonetheless, Jevons was up for the challenge. "A unit of pleasure or pain is difficult even to conceive," he wrote, "but it is the amount of these feelings which is continually prompting us to buying and selling, borrowing and lending, laboring and resting, producing and consuming; and it is from the quantitative effects of the feelings that we must estimate their comparative amounts." While his estimations were necessarily imperfect, they were still a vital step forward in bringing the rigor of mathematics to bear on the often vaguely abstract tradition of economics.

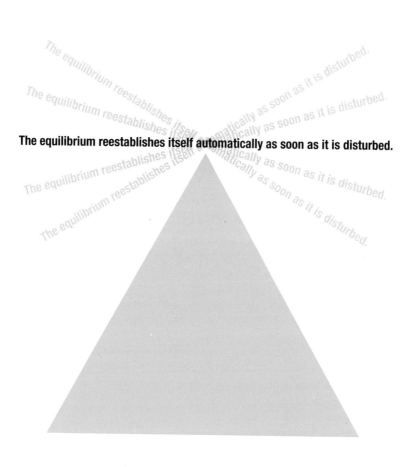

The equilibrium reestablishes itself automatically as soon as it is disturbed.

LEON WALRAS

1834–1910

SOURCE: *Éléments d'économie politique pure*
DATE: 1874
FIELD: Supply and demand

General equilibrium theory seeks to explore the relationship between supply, demand, and price within an economy as a whole (taking into account the various markets active within it). Leon Walras carried out much pivotal work in this area, using complex mathematics to show how the economy as a whole (and not just individual markets) has a tendency to equilibrium—in other words, if there is an excess of demand or supply across an economy, changing prices will rapidly regulate a return to balance.

His work took up a challenge set by his fellow French economist and mathematician Antoine Augustin Cournot, who doubted whether it was provable that the tendency to equilibrium in an individual market could be proven to apply to the economy as a whole. Using simultaneous equations, Walras sought to show how if there was excess demand in any one market, there must be corresponding negative demand in another.

Many others have built upon Walras's work, with efforts ongoing to prove general equilibrium taking into account an almost endless set of variables. However, the theory has its critics too. Some argue that the process of reestablishing equilibrium is excessively long and arduous and does not give due recognition to the causes or impacts of economic crises. As John Maynard Keynes put it: "The long run is a misleading guide to current affairs. In the long run we are all dead. Economists set themselves too easy, too useless a task if in tempestuous seasons they can only tell us that when the storm is past the ocean is flat again."

In gambling, the many must lose in order that the few may win.

27

GEORGE BERNARD SHAW

1856–1950

SOURCE: *Fabian Essays in Socialism*
DATE: 1884
FIELD: Speculation

Best known as one of the greatest playwrights in the English language, George Bernard Shaw was also a dedicated socialist and a founder of the London School of Economics.

His quotation opposite draws a striking parallel between gambling—which in the Victorian era was widely considered a serious threat to the social fabric, mostly afflicting the poorest in society—and the competition encouraged by the capitalist system. In both cases, he argued, the success of the few is reliant on the failure of the many—a position he found abhorrent. To explain his position, he built an analogy based on the land and the treasures that it offers up—some more valuable than others (he cited cabbages and diamonds as extreme examples). "Men," he noted, "come greatly to desire that these capricious gifts of Nature might be intercepted by some agency having the power and the goodwill to distribute them according to the labour done by each in the collective search for them. This desire is socialism…." In contrast, he continued, "the gambling spirit urges man to allow no rival to come between his private individual powers and Step-mother Earth, but rather to secure some acres of her and take his chance of getting diamonds instead of cabbages. This is private property or Unsocialism."

Shaw's message was clear—the desire of the gambler (the epitome of the property-owning, capitalist philosophy) to expand his own wealth at the expense of others is detrimental to the good of society. Moreover, in his pursuit of wealth, he may find himself cast among the impoverished, unlucky majority.

The man who
dies thus rich
dies disgraced.

28

ANDREW CARNEGIE
1835–1919

SOURCE: "Wealth"
DATE: 1889
FIELD: Philanthropy

Born in Scotland, Andrew Carnegie emigrated with his family to the USA as a child and made his fortune from the booming steel industry. By the turn of the 20th century he was among the world's richest people, with a fortune close to half a billion dollars at the time. However, in the years leading up to his death he gave away as much as 90 percent of his wealth to good causes— encompassing educational establishments (including the Carnegie Mellon University and a large number of libraries), research, culture (for example, New York's famous Carnegie Hall), and peace initiatives.

The quotation here comes from an article, "Wealth," that appeared in *The North American Review*, and which was later republished as the stand-alone *The Gospel of Wealth*. In it, he asserted his belief that wealthy capitalists have a moral duty to use their riches to fund cultural and social programs for the improvement of the wider world.

Believing that governments should play a limited role in the economy and that wealth accrues from dedicated hard work, he nonetheless condemned those who lavish their riches upon themselves (and especially those who squander their inherited wealth). Moreover, he was suspicious of simply donating wealth to charitable causes that might themselves make poor use of the funds. Instead, he envisaged a model of philanthropy in which wealthy individuals actively reinvest their wealth into the communities from which it originates, thus creating opportunities for new wealth creation. Money might thus be recirculated through society—and this is a model that has resonated with the new generation of Silicon Valley billionaires.

What made women's labor particularly attractive to the capitalists was not only its lower price but also the greater *submissiveness* **of women**

29

CLARA ZETKIN
1857–1933

SOURCE: Speech at the International Workers' Congress in Paris
DATE: 1889
FIELD: Labor

Clara Zetkin had been an important figure in German socialism since the 1870s, as well as a campaigner for universal suffrage and women's rights. She believed that socialism was pivotal to securing a better deal for women, claiming it was the only economic system that truly served the needs of working-class women. Feminism as a philosophical position was, she contended, the preserve of the middle- and upper-class only.

Drawn to socialism's credo of inherent equality, by contrast she saw capitalism as consolidating inequality. Therefore, she deemed the ostensibly positive step of increased female employment as actually a negative, since, she said, it was used as a tool of capitalism to suppress the labor force as a whole. "The capitalists speculate on the two following factors," she claimed. "The female worker must be paid as poorly as possible and the competition of female labor must be employed to lower the wages of male workers as much as possible. In the same manner the capitalists use child labor to depress women's wages and the work of machines to depress all human labor."

Zetkin's views were influenced by the teachings of August Bebel, a founder of the Social Democratic Workers' Party of Germany and, later, chairman of the Social Democratic Party. He insisted that the goal of socialists was "not only to achieve equality of men and women under the present social order, which constitutes the sole aim of the bourgeois women's movement, but to go far beyond this and to remove all barriers that make one human being dependent upon another, which includes the dependence of one sex upon another."

Economics is a study
of mankind in the ordinary
business of life.

30

ALFRED MARSHALL

1842–1924

SOURCE: *Principles of Economics*
DATE: 1890
FIELD: Neoclassical economics

One of the outstanding economic theorists of his generation, Alfred Marshall was the author of *Principles of Economics*, which became a standard textbook for decades to come. While embracing a scientific and mathematical approach to economic analysis, he also recognized it as a social science—that is to say, a study of human society, human behavior, and human relationships ("the study of mankind in the ordinary business of life"). Economics, he said, "examines that part of individual and social action which is most closely connected with the attainment and with the use of material requisites of well-being."

Marshall did not claim that economics looks at human life and social interactions in their entirety—for instance, he regarded politics and religion as beyond the scope of the discipline. Instead, he believed its role was to examine a vital but narrow part of existence—humanity's pursuit (as individuals and as societies) of material welfare. He was not, though, without his critics. Such eminent figures as Lionel Robbins thought he had reduced the scope of economics too far, and that concepts such as welfare are too vague and subjective to be truly useful.

Nonetheless, Marshall's formulation of what economics is proved hugely influential to generations of economists and students to come. "Man's character has been moulded by his every-day work, and the material resources which he thereby procures, more than by any other influence unless it be that of his religious ideals," he wrote, continuing, "and the two great forming agencies of the world's history have been the religious and the economic."

What is a cynic? A man who knows the price of everything and the value of nothing.

31

OSCAR WILDE
1854–1900

SOURCE: *Lady Windermere's Fan*
DATE: 1892
FIELD: Value

Oscar Wilde—author, playwright, poet, esthete, and provocateur—scripted the quotation here in a conversation between two characters in his play, *Lady Windemere's Fan*. More than merely another example of Wilde's *bons mots*, though, it points the way toward one of the fundamental questions of economics—a conundrum that continues to inspire much debate: How may we measure value?

In broad terms, value in the economics context is effectively the measure of benefit that an economic actor derives from a specific good or service. It is often measured in terms of money, with value being considered equivalent to the maximum expenditure an individual is willing to pay out for the good or service in question. Yet there are myriad problems with this interpretation. For instance, the monetary figure may exceed the price that the market will brook. A glass of tap water may cost just a few pennies (its market price), yet its value to someone who has just completed a marathon is likely much higher. Value is thus subject to a large number of factors that vary wildly over time and from place to place.

Other interpretations equate value to the amount of labor a good or service saves for the purchaser, or how much discomfort it eliminates. Karl Marx, meanwhile, believed the value of a product ought to take into account the volume of labor required to produce it. In truth, like Wilde's cynic, perhaps none of us can truly claim to know the value of anything.

Conspicuous consumption of valuable goods is a means of reputability.

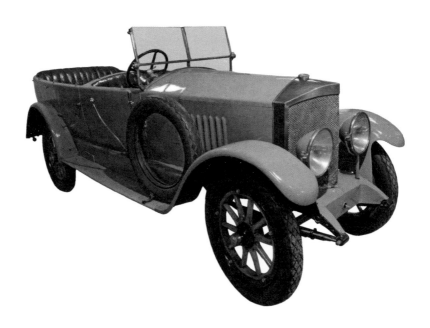

32

THORSTEIN VEBLEN

1857–1929

SOURCE: *The Theory of the Leisure Class*
DATE: 1899
FIELD: Consumerism

Thorstein Veblen popularized the theory of conspicuous consumption—
the phenomenon whereby goods and services are purchased primarily to
emphasize the buyer's wealth and social position—during America's Gilded Age
(ca. 1870s-1900). It was a time when super-rich dynasties, among them the
Rockefellers, Guggenheims, and Vanderbilts, flaunted their vast wealth built
upon industries such as steel and the railways.

According to traditional economic theory, consumers purchase goods and
services to feel the satisfaction of consuming the particular product. But Veblen
saw something different in the growing tide of consumerism sweeping across
American society. As well as utility (that is to say, the satisfaction generated by
a product), he noticed that many economic transactions were enacted to
emphasize the buyer's elevated social status and, by logical extension, the lower
status of others. According to Veblen, consumption is often as much an act of
egoism as one designed to satisfy a specific want or need. "So soon as the
possession of property becomes the basis of popular esteem," he wrote, "[…] it
becomes also a requisite to the complacency which we call self-respect." Nor
did he believe the phenomenon was restricted to the rich—all classes can
partake in it, wherever there is someone with a status of their own to elevate
and the status of another to suppress.

By showing how consumers are subject to an array of social and psychological
influences when making economic decisions, Veblen thus posed a fundamental
challenge to the long-held notion of the rational economic actor that
underpinned so much of classical and neoclassical economics.

God helps those who help themselves.

33

MAX WEBER

1864–1920

SOURCE: *The Protestant Ethic and the Spirit of Capitalism*
DATE: 1905
FIELD: Economic sociology

The Protestant Ethic and the Spirit of Capitalism is recognized as one of the first great texts of economic sociology—a term coined by Stanley Jevons for the study of the social causes and effects of economic activity.

Max Weber's work was in part a response to the writings of Karl Marx, which argued that human history (including its religious institutions) is molded by economic phenomena. Weber, by contrast, was seeking to show that economic thought (and specifically, capitalism) emerges at least to some extent out of social and religious circumstances. Nonetheless, he wrote that "It is, of course, not my aim to substitute for a one-sided materialistic an equally one-sided spiritualistic causal interpretation of culture and history."

Adam Smith had earlier attempted to address the relationship between economics and religion—for instance, pondering whether religion fosters a climate of trust and self-regulation that reduces risk and so facilitates economic activity. But Weber took things on several stages with his analysis of economic development in various countries from the 16th to the 19th centuries. He concluded that Protestant nations had an advantage over their Catholic counterparts because Protestantism nurtured a work ethic and culture of frugality vital to the development of capitalism. Believing in predestination, he suggested, Protestants worked diligently as a means of exhibiting their virtue, refusing luxuries in favor of reinvesting their wealth. Catholics, meanwhile, are suspicious of profit-motivated business since their route to salvation rests in doing "good works." Controversial and widely disputed, Weber's work nonetheless opened up a startling new area of economic analysis and dialogue.

Communism [emerges] when unpaid work for the common good becomes the general phenomenon.

34

VLADIMIR LENIN

1870-1924

SOURCE: *Selected Works* (Volume VIII)
DATE: 1905
FIELD: Communism

Though Marx died with his dreams of establishing a communist utopia unfulfilled, Vladimir Lenin founded the world's first communist state after the overthrow of the ruling Romanov family in Russia in 1917. Lenin thus found himself in the unique position of translating Marx's radical theories into practice, forging a society that went far beyond the low-level socialism that had found limited expression in a few European nations. "If we were to ask ourselves in what way Communism differs from Socialism," he wrote, "we would have to reply that Socialism is the society which grows directly out of capitalism, that it is the first form of the new society. Communism, on the other hand, is a higher form of society which can develop only when Socialism has taken firm hold."

According to Lenin, socialism implies the performance of work without the aid of capitalism while retaining many of the trappings of capitalism—for instance, accounting, supervision, and worker compensation. These are, he suggested, remnants of capitalism to which we have become habituated. "All these run counter to a real Communist economy," he argued. "Communism [...] is the name we apply to a system under which people become accustomed to the performance of public duties without any specific machinery of compulsion."

Of course, history shows that the Communist experiment in Russia was to be highly problematic. Famine, fear, and autocracy became hallmarks of the Soviet Union in the 20th century as the vision of Lenin (and indeed Marx) crumbled in the face of human frailty and economic mismanagement. Yet for all its failures, communism could claim to have fundamentally changed the world.

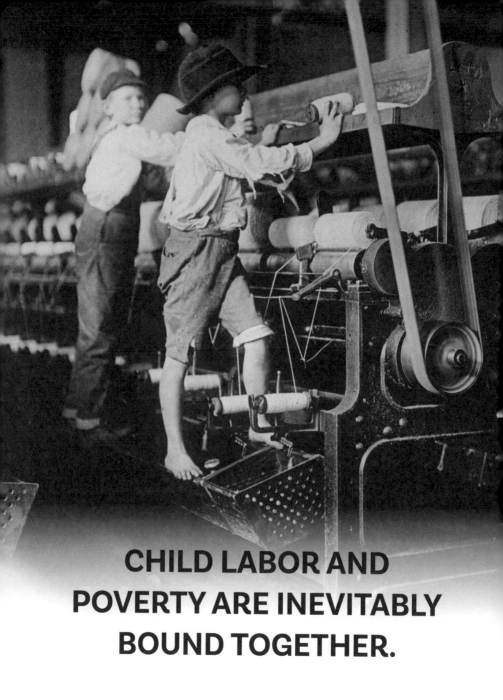

CHILD LABOR AND
POVERTY ARE INEVITABLY
BOUND TOGETHER.

35

GRACE ABBOTT
1878–1939

SOURCE: Public speech
DATE: ca. 1910
FIELD: Child labor

An academic and social reformer, Abbott made her name fighting against the exploitation of immigrant workers. However, she is best known today for her stance against child labor. Such was her standing that she was appointed head of the Department Against Child Labor in the US Children's Bureau, an agency founded in 1912 by President Woodrow Wilson to protect the "right to childhood." She then served as director of the Children's Office in the US Department of Labor from 1921 until 1934.

Abbott campaigned tirelessly for the rights of, variously, immigrant, women, and child laborers, emphasizing how each was particularly vulnerable to exploitation. She realized that short-term pressures to earn an income, often vital to the very survival of their families, militated against members of these groups realizing their full long-term economic potential. In the case of children, she was highly critical of the situation that saw children earn lowly pay in menial factory jobs even as their work deprived them of the chance to gain the education that would vastly improve their earning potential in adulthood. This was a prime example, she argued, of how child labor consolidated poverty among many families.

Her efforts at practical reform included championing the 1916 Keating–Owen Child Labor Act, the provisions of which included a ban on the sale of goods from factories employing under-14s. Passed by Congress, it was overturned by the Supreme Court in 1918. Despite such setbacks, Abbott played a vital role in shining a light into some of the darker corners of modern American economics.

In general, industrialists are interested [...] only in the private, net product of their operations.

36

ARTHUR PIGOU
1877–1959

SOURCE: *The Economics of Welfare*
DATE: 1920
FIELD: Welfare

A disciple of Alfred Marshall, Arthur Pigou carried out his most influential work in the field of welfare economics—as he put it, "that part of social welfare that can be brought directly or indirectly into relation with the measuring rod of money." In particular, he developed Marshall's ideas surrounding externalities. An externality is a cost imposed or a benefit enjoyed by an outside party that has not been taken into account by the primary economic actor in any given situation.

As Pigou observed, industrialists are typically more concerned with their own business and its finances than the economic implications of their actions on external parties. For instance, a business owner powering a factory by burning fossil fuels may cause an array of environmental problems that it falls to third parties to rectify. The local council is responsible for the upkeep of buildings dirtied by smoke, the local hospital must look after the child whose asthma has been exacerbated by poor air quality, while the national government undertakes initiatives to combat the threat of global warming, and so on.

Pigou contended that government intervention is justified where externalities exist. Factory owners, for example, may be taxed according to the volume of fossil fuels they burn. The revenue may then be used to address the problems that pollution causes. Such a punitive charge is now known as a Pigovian Tax. On the other hand, the government may offer subsidies to business owners who adopt environmentally friendly practices. Through such a carrot-and-stick approach, Pigou argued, the social cost of externalities may be offset.

In the socialist commonwealth [...] there is only groping in the **dark.**

37

LUDWIG VON MISES

1881–1973

SOURCE: *Economic Calculation in the Socialist Commonwealth*
DATE: 1920
FIELD: Socialism

Ludwig von Mises was a leading figure in the Austrian School of economics, championing liberal values and laissez-faire economics (that is to say, free-market economics unhindered by government intervention). An unstinting believer in individual liberty and a lifelong student of human nature, it is perhaps unsurprising that he was utterly opposed to socialism, which he abhorred for subjugating the individual to the needs of the wider society.

Economic Calculation in the Socialist Commonwealth was regarded by some as the nail in the coffin for socialist ideology. Its author was certainly caustic in his condemnations. "Economics, as such," he said, "figures all too sparsely in the glamorous pictures painted by the [Socialist] Utopians. They invariably explain how, in the cloud-cuckoo lands of their fancy, roast pigeons will in some way fly into the mouths of the comrades, but they omit to show how this miracle is to take place."

In von Mises's estimation, economies are so complex that market prices are vital to gauging profits, which in turn reveal levels of demand—a factor vital in any system of cogent economic planning. But, he noted, socialist societies use money in a limited capacity, to pay wages and purchase consumer goods but not for the purchase of production factors, such as raw materials (since they are provided by the state). Socialist central planners, he argued, thus lack the necessary information to make informed economic choices. "Every economic change," he wrote, "becomes an undertaking whose success can be neither appraised in advance nor later retrospectively determined." "Socialism," he concluded, "is the abolition of rational economy."

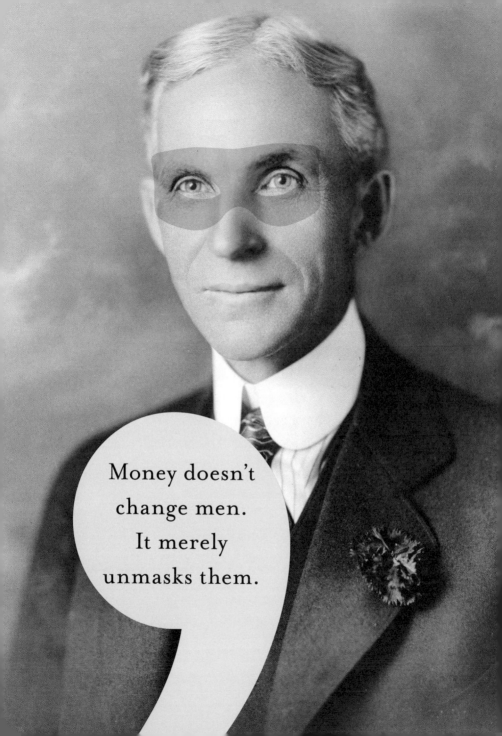

Money doesn't
change men.
It merely
unmasks them.

38

HENRY FORD

HENRY FORD

1863–1947

SOURCE: *The American Magazine*
DATE: 1921
FIELD: Entrepreneurship

Henry Ford, founder of the Ford Motor Company, enjoyed incredible success as an industrialist. Almost single-handedly, he developed systems of mass production (including the assembly line) that ensured the motor car evolved from being a plaything of the rich to becoming a realistic aspiration for millions of ordinary people. By the 1920s, his personal wealth was put at somewhere close to $1.2 billion. However, success had not come effortlessly for him—he helmed several failed businesses before the Ford Model T took off.

Well acquainted with the highs and lows, Ford seems to have had a very sanguine attitude to money. For example, there is a perhaps apocryphal story that his dry cleaner once found an uncashed check for $125,000 in one of Ford's suit pockets. Ford always considered money merely a tool to achieve what one wants, rather than an end in itself. As he told an interviewer in 1922, "Nothing can be made except by makers, nothing can be managed except by managers. Money cannot make anything and money cannot manage anything." On another occasion, he observed that "A business that makes nothing but money is a poor business."

He did nonetheless believe that money accrues to value, so that "Many entrepreneurs achieve financial success because they're playing some essential role in people's lives" before adding that "money isn't the object of the game; it's merely a natural aspect of each transaction." Hence Ford's assertion that money may reveal character, but does not fundamentally change it—give two men a million dollars and the benevolent man will show his inherent generosity, while the avaricious man will confirm his greed.

October 1929

Mon		7	14	21	28
Tues	1	8	15	22	⃝29
Wed	2	9	16	23	30
Thu	3	10	17	24	31
Fri	4	11	18	25	
Sat	5	12	19	26	
Sun	6	13	20	27	

The economists are generally right in their predictions, but generally a good deal out in their dates.

39

SIDNEY WEBB

SIDNEY WEBB

1859–1947

SOURCE: *The Observer* newspaper
DATE: 1924
FIELD: Economic forecasting

Sidney Webb was a socialist and thinker who, along with the likes of his wife Beatrice Webb and such eminent figures as George Bernard Shaw, had turned the Fabian Society (established in 1884) into one of the hotbeds of intellectual debate by the early decades of the 20th century. He was also one of the cofounders of the London School of Economics, as well as a member of parliament for the Labour Party who served variously as President of the Board of Trade, Secretary of State for Dominion Affairs, and Secretary of State for the Colonies.

Webb's view on economic forecasting chimed with the thoughts of another prominent British economist, Sir Alexander Cairncross (1911–98), who observed that "a forecast is never a statement of fact. We know only what is behind us, never what is in front of us." The business of economic forecasting regularly finds itself in disrepute, principally at moments of largely unforeseen crisis. Why, nonforecasters have legitimately asked, did so few forecasters predict, for instance, the Wall Street Crash in the 1920s or the Great Recession that struck in 2007?

Few would disagree that the business of economic forecasting is one fraught with complications. Indeed, the failure of Webb himself and his wife to perceive the serious failings of Stalinist Russia in such works as *Soviet Communism: A New Civilisation?* (1935) and *The Truth About Soviet Russia* (1942) reinforces the view that looking into the economic crystal ball is not a business for the faint-hearted.

Between mathematics, statistics, and economics we find [...] econometrics.

40

RAGNAR FRISCH

1895–1973

SOURCE: *On a Problem in Pure Economics*
DATE: 1926
FIELD: Econometrics

Along with Dutch economist Jan Tinbergen, Ragnar Frisch was the recipient of the first Nobel Memorial Prize in Economic Sciences, awarded in 1969 for "having developed and applied dynamic models for the analysis of economic processes." He is also credited with coining the twin terms "microeconomics" and "macroeconomics" to distinguish between the study of economics at the level of individual actors and at the level of the economy as a whole.

Frisch's great innovation was the development of econometrics, which uses standard mathematical methods (most commonly, statistics) in order to describe and analyze economic systems. Though the term had been in use since 1910 and many of its underlying principles were established by Tinbergen, Frisch is nevertheless regarded as having refined it into a fully functioning academic approach. In his own words, "Econometrics has as its aim to subject abstract laws of theoretical political economy or 'pure' economics to experimental and numerical verification, and thus to turn pure economics, as far as possible, into a science in the strict sense of the word."

Frisch was thus a pivotal figure in striving to remove from economic analysis factors that might be deemed assumption, opinion, or prejudice. In simple terms, the exponent of econometrics seeks economic truth by analyzing data and establishing mathematical relationships. Yet there remains an alternative, powerful school of thought that suggests economics—as a social science—is subject to a host of factors that cannot be grasped by such a coldly scientific approach.

I believe it is a religious duty to get all the money you can, fairly and honestly; to keep all you can, and to give away all you can.

41

JOHN D. ROCKEFELLER, SR.

1839–1937

SOURCE: *TIME* magazine
DATE: 1928
FIELD: Philanthropy

John D. Rockefeller, Sr., was another of those industrialists who made their fortunes during America's fabled Gilded Age in the late 19th century. He had the oil industry to thank for making him not only the richest man in America but, by some measures, the wealthiest individual anywhere in the world in the modern age.

Like several of his Gilded Age counterparts (not least, Andrew Carnegie; see page 61), Rockefeller took immense pleasure first in the accumulation of wealth and then in its philanthropic redistribution. He was notorious for his ruthlessness as a businessman, squeezing his suppliers and rivals so that at his peak he is said to have controlled some 90 percent of the US oil industry. In 1911 he was compelled by the Supreme Court to divide up his company, Standard Oil, having been found guilty of violating antitrust laws. Though he extolled getting money "fairly and honestly," it is fair to say he regularly strayed into gray areas.

Yet while he showed scant regard for his competitors in business, he felt the compulsion to share the benefits of his wealth, with no lesser aim than to promote "the well-being of mankind throughout the world." "I believe the power to make money is a gift of God," he told an interviewer in 1932, "to be developed and used to the best of our ability for the good of mankind [...] according to the dictates of my conscience." In such a way, he established a blueprint for those super-rich individuals who believe they are best placed to decide how their money may be most widely beneficial, independent of the opinions of governments and other established organizations.

Economic competition is not war, but rivalry in mutual service.

42

EDWIN CANNAN

1861–1935

SOURCE: *A Review of Economic Theory*
DATE: 1929
FIELD: Competition

Edwin Cannan was a professor at the London School of Economics from its inception in 1895, and was instrumental in realigning it from its Fabian (ie, socialist) beginnings toward the neoclassical school (with its focus on free-market mechanisms). Over the course of his career, he evolved from an interventionist to an advocate of free-market liberalism.

Living in the post-Darwin age, he was conscious of the idea that competition determines the survival of the fittest and, by extension, the downfall of the weakest. Moreover, he recognized it as a theme regularly revisited in the narrative of human history. "That tribes of mankind have struggled for existence, and that some have been exterminated by others, is doubtless true, though the conquerors, who alone tell the tale, have generally been led by their pride in butchery to exaggerate rather than to conceal the extent of their success in wiping out the enemy," he noted.

But Cannan saw competition in the economic sphere somewhat differently. Competition is, he came to conclude, the method by which all actors within an economy are directed toward their most suitable role. "The pressure which it [competition] exercises is not directed towards the extermination of the 'unfit,'" he contended, "but towards inducing everyone, whether 'fittest' or 'unfittest' to do the kind of work which will pay him best. We say, loosely, that a blind or legless man is at a disadvantage in competition, but such a man has far more chance of being able to support himself by labour in a society of men cooperating by way of competition than he would have in a state of isolation."

Economics brings
into full view that conflict
of choice which is one of the
permanent characteristics
of human existence.

43

LIONEL ROBBINS
1898–1984

SOURCE: *An Essay on the Nature and Significance of Economic Science*
DATE: 1932
FIELD: Opportunity cost

In his *Essay on the Nature and Significance of Economic Science*, Lionel Robbins sought nothing less than to attempt to distill the essence of economics in order to come up with a new, objective definition of the discipline. It is, he concluded, "a science which studies human behaviour as a relationship between ends and scarce means which have alternative uses." It is, in other words, the study of how people behave, given that they cannot have everything they want.

Each time we make an economic decision, we are forced to choose that which we want or need most at the expense of one or more other options that we would also like in an ideal world. What we give up is known as the "opportunity cost"—a term originated by Austrian economist Friedrich von Wieser in 1914 (although the concept had been partially explored by several earlier economists). When we pay the insurance on our car, the opportunity cost might, for instance, be the holiday we might otherwise have had, or that new carpet for the bedroom. For Robbins, opportunity cost is at the very crux of the "conflict of choice" that marks out the daily life of our species.

It was in part because of this sense that every gain is accompanied by a loss that Robbins described the economist as "a true tragedian."

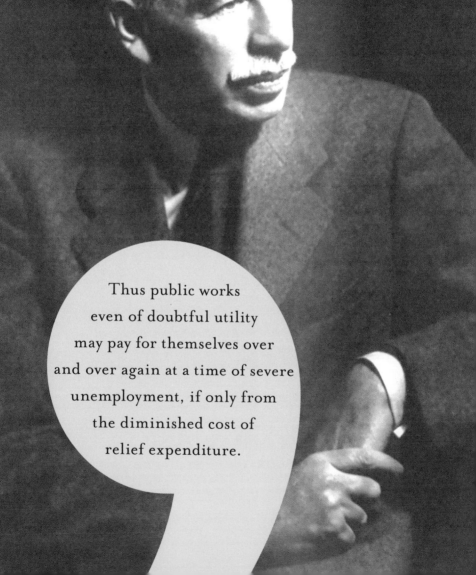

Thus public works
even of doubtful utility
may pay for themselves over
and over again at a time of severe
unemployment, if only from
the diminished cost of
relief expenditure.

44

1883–1946

SOURCE: *The General Theory of Employment, Interest and Money*
DATE: 1936
FIELD: Keynesianism

With his *General Theory of Employment, Interest and Money*, John Maynard Keynes helped to mold macroeconomic theory across much of the developed world for a significant portion of the 20th century. As he told George Bernard Shaw in 1935: "I believe myself to be writing a book on economic theory which will largely revolutionize [...] the way the world thinks about its economic problems."

Writing at the height of the Great Depression, Keynes sought to turn the received wisdom of classical economics on its head. As he saw the human toll that mass unemployment was exacting across the globe, he challenged the orthodoxy that free markets left to themselves will return to a state of equilibrium in the long run, bringing with it a return to full (or near-full) employment. Instead, he argued, economic recovery is more readily effected by increasing aggregate demand—in other words, governments can spend their way out of recession.

He urged governments to invest money (secured on credit if need be) in large-scale infrastructure projects. By doing so, a market is created that encourages employers to take on new labor, which in turn has more money to spend and so further bolsters the market. Moreover, the wider population reaps the benefits of new infrastructure. Keynesianism was enthusiastically taken up by world governments during the Great Depression and in the aftermath of the Second World War. And although his views had largely fallen out of favor by the 1970s, they were met with renewed interest in light of the Great Recession of the 2000s.

Economic progress, in capitalist society, means turmoil.

45

JOSEPH SCHUMPETER

1883–1950

SOURCE: *Capitalism, Socialism and Democracy*
DATE: 1942
FIELD: Creative destruction

Joseph Schumpeter's most famous contribution to economics is the concept of "creative destruction"—the counterintuitive notion that recessions are forces for economic good because they rid the market of inefficient actors and create space for innovative growth. One innovator inexorably follows another, refining their business model to the point that they may wrest dominant market position from the incumbent. On the basis of this philosophy, Schumpeter was vehemently opposed to any state intervention in the economy.

Describing creative destruction as "the essential fact about capitalism," he took a diametrically opposed view to Karl Marx. Where Marx saw economic crises as the undesirable but inevitable consequence of capitalism's continual need to overturn the existing economic order, Schumpeter argued the crises are key to human progress. History suggests he may have a point. The Industrial Revolution with its myriad innovations can be viewed as a prime example of creative destruction, replacing old, inefficient businesses with bold new ones. Others cite the rise of the Internet as another example, killing off, for example, long-established retail businesses, newspaper publishers, and record companies, but creating an environment in which new ways of selling and sharing media may thrive.

Yet even though creative destruction may usher in a brave new world of sorts, others worry about the price that is paid. Where the cycle of destruction and renewal brings about periods of recession and depression, what becomes of the subsumed business owners and their workers while the new business models establish their foothold?

A POLICY OF FREEDOM FOR THE INDIVIDUAL IS THE ONLY TRULY PROGRESSIVE POLICY.

46

FRIEDRICH HAYEK

1899–1992

SOURCE: *The Road to Serfdom*
DATE: 1944
FIELD: Spontaneous order

Friedrich Hayek was a leading figure in the Austrian School of economics, which covers a broad range of opinion loosely united around the belief that the free market, for all its faults, most efficiently allocates scarce resources. However, it doubts the existence of informed, rational economic actors. Instead, it believes the market assimilates data from the multitude of transactions that takes place within it (irrespective of whether a transaction is of itself rational or irrational) to ensure the correct level of supply at the right price. As Hayek put it, "There exist orderly structures which are the product of the action of many men but are not the result of human design." This idea is at the crux of his concept of spontaneous order.

As such, Hayek was one of the most outspoken critics of the prevailing tendency toward Keynesianism at the time he wrote *The Road to Serfdom*. Government intervention, he contended, threatened the phenomenon of spontaneous order, since no government could hope to record and analyze the quantity of data necessary for the markets to function correctly. This was even more the case, he suggested, in a totalitarian state, where power resides with an individual or small group. The role of the state should be limited, he said, to protecting those mechanisms that allow the free market to function. Regarded as an "outsider" to the economic establishment in his own lifetime, his ideas would gain credibility from the 1970s, when they were championed by the likes of Milton Friedman (see page 129).

This theory of games of strategy is the proper instrument with which to develop a theory of economic behavior.

47

JOHN VON NEUMANN / OSKAR MORGENSTERN
1903-1957 / 1902-1977

SOURCE: *Theory of Games and Economic Behavior*
DATE: 1944
FIELD: Game theory

Oskar Morgenstern, an economist, teamed up with mathematician John von Neumann to create their landmark study applying the nascent field of game theory to economics. Their aim was to look at how the actions of specific economic actors (for instance, governments and market-leading companies) affect the workings of markets and economies. They mathematically analyzed a number of theoretical zero-sum games (typically featuring two participants, one of whom will emerge the winner and one the loser) in a bid to establish general rules as to how we go about making decisions when forced to consider the likely actions of others.

In each case, they made certain presumptions—for instance, that the preferences of each actor remained constant, that they could sensibly evaluate their own best interests, that they comprehended all the available options, and that they always sought to maximize their interests. Their work further undermined the notion of the rational economic actor and also increased interest in how psychological factors influence economic decisions.

In the 1950s the brilliant mathematician John Nash built upon their work, moving beyond zero-sum games to scenarios where multiple agents make decisions independently of each other. He came up with what is now known as Nash equilibrium, whereby situations exist in which no agent has an incentive to reconsider their course of action regardless of the strategies chosen by the other agents. Today, game theory has moved outward from the economic realm to a host of other real-world fields, guiding everything from political strategy and industrial relations to health policy and advertising.

We must not tolerate oppressive government or industrial oligarchy in the form of monopolies and cartels.

48

HENRY A. WALLACE

1888–1965

SOURCE: "The Danger of American Fascism" in *The New York Times*
DATE: 1944
FIELD: Monopolies

Henry A. Wallace, who was US vice-president between 1941 and 1945, was by inclination a liberal (his political career saw him affiliated with both the Republican and Democratic parties, and he also founded the Progressive Party). He had strongly supported President Roosevelt's New Deal in the 1930s—a package of economic reforms and public works programs designed to counter the effects of the Great Depression. As the Second World War raged, he wrote a coruscating attack on fascism, from which the quotation opposite is taken. He highlighted the fascist tendency to manipulate truth for its own ends, to depict social "others" as the enemy, and to promote intolerance and totalitarianism in the name of the public good.

In the economic sphere, he fixed his gaze on those figures in industry willing to support fascist programs for their own financial interests. He suggested that "monopolists" by their nature fear the competition of the free market and in pursuit of eliminating rivals were prepared to sacrifice democracy—the "free market" of politics, as it were—in favor of fascistic regimes. In order to overcome fascism, Wallace argued, it was essential that economies be open and efficient but also inclusive and fair. "Democracy, to crush fascism internally," he wrote, "must demonstrate its capacity to 'make the trains run on time,'"— echoing Mussolini's famous boast in Italy. "It must develop the ability to keep people fully employed and at the same time balance the budget. It must put human beings first and dollars second. It must appeal to reason and decency and not to violence and deceit."

Economic problems have no sharp edges. They shade off imperceptibly into politics, sociology, and ethics.

49

KENNETH BOULDING

1910–1993

SOURCE: *The Economics of Peace*
DATE: 1945
FIELD: Economics as a social science

Kenneth Boulding was a prolific economist and philosopher, who believed that economics as an academic discipline is part of a wider social science and needs to be seen within the broader context of human psychology and modes of social organization. He made his name in the early 1940s with *Economic Analysis*, which was destined to become a standard textbook, and published *The Economics of Peace* at the end of the Second World War. As he put it, "It is hardly an exaggeration to say that the ultimate answer to every economic problem lies in some other field." He regarded economics as the "skeleton of social science" which might collapse into a "jellyfish of casual observation and speculation" without the "flesh and blood" provided by other fields of study.

His fear that too many economists risk losing themselves within their own narrow bands of interest was only accentuated in the postwar period, when the pressure to rebuild wrecked economies was intense. He warned against framing "elegant systems for world reconstruction" if there was little chance of practically enacting them, given particular political, social, and psychological realities. As he put it: "Economics of itself is too rational a science to be realistic, for reality in the human sphere is very far from rational. It is not enough, therefore, to give an intellectual solution for the world's economic problems; we must indicate how, from the existing state of war and confusion, men may pass to a better world by steps which are possible under the present framework of beliefs, ideas, and organizations."

The art of economics consists in looking not merely at the immediate but at the longer effects of any act or policy.

50

HENRY HAZLITT
1894–1993

SOURCE: *Economics in One Lesson*
DATE: 1946
FIELD: Economic forecasting

An esteemed economics journalist, Henry Hazlitt's *Economics in One Lesson* espoused a traditionally conservative, laissez-faire philosophy. A staunch critic of Keynes, his quotation here may be seen as the antithesis of Keynes's argument that the markets should not be left to restore their own equilibrium over the longer term. Where Keynes warned against overlooking the short- to mid-term outlook (as he so memorably put it, "In the long run we are all dead"), Hazlitt believed the long-term view is vital. He would go so far as to accuse Keynes's greatest work, *The General Theory of Employment, Interest and Money*, of containing not "a single doctrine that is both true and original. What is original in the book is not true; and what is true is not original."

There is, Hazlitt complained, "the persistent tendency of men to see only the immediate effects of a given policy, or its effects only on a special group, and to neglect to inquire what the long-run effects of that policy will be not only on that special group but on all groups." Failure to properly assess the likely long-term effects was, he wrote, "the whole difference between good economics and bad. The bad economist sees only what immediately strikes the eye; the good economist also looks beyond. The bad economist sees only the direct consequences of a proposed course; the good economist looks also at the longer and indirect consequences." "Today," he observed portentously, "is already the tomorrow which the bad economist yesterday urged us to ignore."

The earth provides enough to satisfy every man's need
but not for every man's greed.

51

MOHANDAS GANDHI
1869–1948

SOURCE: *Mahatma Gandhi: The Last Phase* by Pyarelal Nayyar (1958)
DATE: ca. 1947
FIELD: Inequality

As the leader of India's independence movement during the period of British rule, Mohandas Gandhi emerged as one of the great sociopolitical figures of the 20th century. A champion of peaceful civil disobedience, he campaigned passionately for economic and social equality—a sensitive subject in a country divided along strict caste lines. As revealed in this quotation—cited by Pyarelal Nayyar, his one-time personal secretary and later his biographer—Gandhi regarded poverty not as an inevitable phenomenon but an avoidable result of human greed.

Writing in 1938 in the weekly journal *Harijan*, Gandhi proclaimed: "I want to bring about an equalization of status. The working classes have all these centuries been isolated and relegated to a lower status [...] I want to allow no differentiation between the son of a weaver, of an agriculturist and of a schoolmaster."

It was a subject he would return to time and again, although he was keen to avoid accusations of economic naivety. In 1946 he wrote that the "economic equality of my conception does not mean that everyone will literally have the same amount. It simply means that everybody should have enough for his or her needs. The real meaning of economic equality is 'To each according to his need.' [...] If a single man demands as much as a man with wife and four children, that will be a violation of economic equality. Let no one try to justify the glaring difference between the classes and the masses, the prince and the pauper, by saying that the former need more. That will be idle sophistry and a travesty of my argument."

Everyone has the right to a standard of living adequate for the health and well-being of himself and of his family.

52

UNIVERSAL DECLARATION OF HUMAN RIGHTS

UNIVERSAL DECLARATION OF HUMAN RIGHTS

1948

SOURCE: The United Nations
DATE: 1948
FIELD: Economic rights

In the aftermath of the Second World War, the United Nations set up a Commission on Human Rights that drafted the Universal Declaration of Human Rights. Adopted in 1948, it was conceived as a document enshrining the basic rights to which all citizens of every nation are entitled. As such, it has provided a blueprint for legal systems throughout the world, although the Declaration itself possessed moral rather than legal authority until 1976, when the International Covenant on Civil and Political Rights was enacted.

The Declaration echoed the "Four Freedoms" elucidated in President Franklin Roosevelt's 1941 State of the Union address, one of which was "freedom from want." The quotation opposite comes from Article 25 of the Declaration, which specifically references food, clothing, housing, medical care, and "necessary social services." It also decrees the "right to security in the event of unemployment, sickness, disability, widowhood, old age or other lack of livelihood in circumstances beyond his control"—a reaffirming of Article 23's "right to social security."

It economic terms, the Declaration is a remarkable milestone in human history. Never before had an attempt been made to specify the moral economic entitlement of all human beings, including the right to receive support from the state in times of need. Adopted by 48 nations in 1948, among the notable abstentions were the Soviet Union, several of its Eastern Bloc neighbors, and South Africa. Nonetheless, rarely had such a significant document secured such widespread support across the globe.

**GIVE ME A ONE-HANDED ECONOMIST.
ALL MY ECONOMISTS SAY,
ON THE ONE HAND... ON THE OTHER...**

53

HARRY S. TRUMAN
1884–1972

SOURCE: Hearings before the Subcommittee on International Trade,
Investment, and Monetary Policy, House of Representatives (1976)
DATE: ca. 1950
FIELD: Economic advice

President from 1945 until 1953, Harry S. Truman served during a period of
rapid postwar reconstruction. It was he, for instance, who oversaw
implementation of the Marshall Plan that rebuilt Western Europe's ravaged
economies. Meanwhile, at home, he phased out the wage and price controls
that had been in force during the war and ushered in a period of growth
unprecedented in American history that established the USA as a superpower.

Yet while ultimate responsibility for economic policy lay with Truman, he was
able to consult with the elite economic thinkers of his time. In 1946 he
established the Council of Economic Advisers, charged with providing the
president with objective analysis of economic questions at both the domestic
and international levels. It was the first time that the Oval Office had been able
to call on such an institution, having previously gotten its advice in a far less
formal way. Yet, inevitably, the Council members often disagreed among
themselves. In 1949, for example, the chairman resigned after falling out with
a fellow councillor as to whether the government should expand its defense
budget. While some believed the government could sustain a deficit during
those boom years, others feared it would lead to a decline in domestic living
standards. It was such disagreements, perhaps, that prompted the president's
memorable outburst.

Truman's frustrations remain just as pertinent today. One might look at, say,
the disagreement over the use of fiscal stimuli in the wake of the Great
Recession to see that economists rarely agree.

54

1893–1976

SOURCE: *Quotations from Chairman Mao Zedong* (1964)
DATE: 1955
FIELD: Socialism

Chairman Mao was the communist revolutionary leader who oversaw the establishment of the People's Republic of China, over which he ruled with an iron fist from 1949 until his death in 1976. He is the source of the economic and philosophical worldview that has come to be known as Maoism. His quotation here hints at the fanatical fervor with which he embraced his project of national renewal, as well as his belief that he carried the will of his people with him. As his increasingly autocratic rule illustrated, he had little time for his opponents. "Those who can only follow the old routine in a revolutionary period are utterly incapable of seeing this enthusiasm," he wrote. "They are blind and all is dark ahead of them. At times they go so far as to confound right and wrong and turn things upside down […] Such people are always passive, always fail to move forward at the critical moment, and always have to be given a shove in the back before they move a step."

Yet, as history would show, it was Mao himself who struggled to readjust his thinking in the face of overwhelming evidence that he was on the wrong path. In 1957, for example, he embarked on the Great Leap Forward—a program of rapid industrialization in the traditionally agrarian country—that resulted in devastating famine and the deaths of tens of millions of citizens. His words opposite serve as a warning of what can happen when people of power become unbendingly wedded to particular economic philosophies, regardless of the practical realities of the world in which they function.

Capitalism is too complicated a system for a newly independent nation. Hence the need for a socialistic society.

55

1909–1972

SOURCE: *Ghana: The Autobiography of Kwame Nkrumah*
DATE: 1957
FIELD: Development economics

Kwame Nkrumah was a revolutionary who led the Gold Coast to independence from the United Kingdom in 1957, whereupon he served first as prime minister and then as president of the nation now renamed as Ghana. His rule was hugely controversial, taking on an increasingly authoritarian air until he was removed in a coup in 1966 as the economy collapsed around him. Yet in recognition of the earlier part of his career, he remains a pivotal figure in the movement for Pan-African unity that swept across the continent in the aftermath of the Second World War. In economic terms, he favored a socialist approach to spur postcolonial economic development—a system that seemed to fit well with the communal social structures that had characterized much of precolonial Africa. Moreover, large parts of the continent had little in the way of a tradition of private property, that being one of the underpinning features of Western capitalism.

Yet the Africa-specific form of socialism that Nkrumah envisaged struggled from the outset. Attempts to accelerate industrialization, coupled with falling global cocoa prices, left the agricultural sector in a weakened state. Meanwhile, spiraling international debt forced him to raise taxes while the population faced food shortages—and all the while endemic corruption thwarted countless well-intentioned schemes. Confronted by increasingly vocal critics, Nkrumah became ever more hardline in his approach, banning opposition parties and imprisoning rivals until his overthrow. Where once Ghana had represented a beacon of hope for postcolonial Africa, Nkrumah left a country emblematic of many of the problems the continent as a whole faced in the second half of the 20th century.

Inflation is like sin: every government denounces it and every government practices it.

56

SIR FREDERICK WILLIAM LEITH-ROSS
1887–1968

SOURCE: *The Observer* newspaper
DATE: 1957
FIELD: Inflation

Sir Frederick William Leith-Ross was the UK government's chief economic adviser from 1932 until the end of the Second World War. He was also strongly of the opinion that, contrary to the ideas of John Maynard Keynes and the like, the government could not inject life into the wider economy by increasing its spending. Indeed, he believed that government inputs had no impact in increasing overall economic activity, since government spending only serves to crowd out equivalent levels of private spending.

However, Leith-Ross understood that in the real world, politicians make promises to electorates that demand high levels of spending. Moreover, he lived in an era when administrations around the world responded to depressed global economic conditions by trying to spend their way out of trouble—funding works in the hope of creating jobs, in turn spurring consumer spending (since there would be additional workers with money in their pockets) and so energizing the economy as a whole. He also recognized that this often causes problems of its own. As spending increases, suppliers raise their prices (that is to say, inflation occurs) until demand is dampened, producers lose confidence, jobs are shed, and prices fall again.

For much of the 20th century—until the 1970s, when the ideas of Milton Friedman came to hold sway in many developed economies—it was believed that inflation was the inevitable payoff for having elevated rates of employment. Hence Leith-Ross's observation here that while governments typically understood the dangers of inflation to the long-term economic outlook, they nonetheless felt compelled to dabble in it.

Economic growth without social progress lets the great majority of people remain in poverty, while a privileged few reap the benefits of rising abundance.

57

JOHN F. KENNEDY
1917–1963

SOURCE: Address to Congress
DATE: 1961
FIELD: Inequality

The youthful and charismatic John F. Kennedy won the 1960 US presidential election on a platform of social progressiveness. However, while hopes among many were high, the economy he inherited from his predecessor, Dwight D. Eisenhower, was in a moribund state. Kennedy promised state intervention in a bid to reverse the recession in which the country was mired. He vowed to loosen the purse strings to, as he famously put it, "get this country moving again"—funding, for instance, an urban renewal program and investment in depressed rural areas, while using monetary policy to keep interest rates low.

His plan seemed to work pretty well, too—GDP grew by over 5 percent between 1961 and 1963. Yet Kennedy never lost sight of the fact that his nation's post-Second World War boom (for growth had been robust for most of that period) was not reflected in better living conditions for all. As he noted in his Inaugural Address in January 1961: "If a free society cannot help the many who are poor, it cannot save the few who are rich." In his brief tenure at the White House, he thus introduced a swathe of social security benefit reforms and raised the minimum wage. As the world emerged from the shadow of war and America took its place as a superpower, Kennedy represented the hopes of a generation who believed that economic prosperity could be allied with social progressiveness. His assassination in November 1963 ensured much of his project would never be finished, although he remains a potent symbol of faith in economic and social equality.

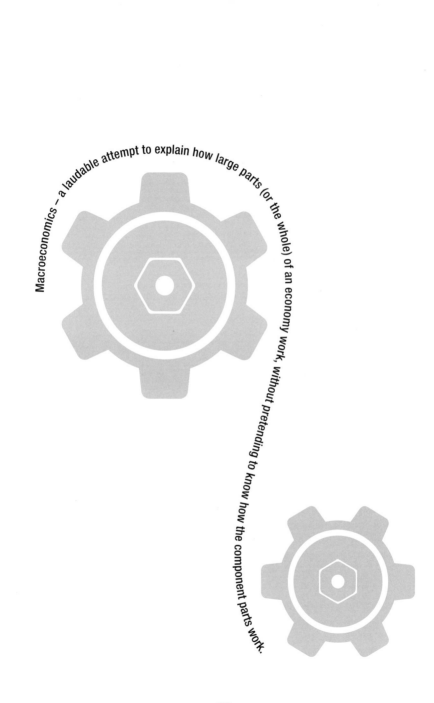

Macroeconomics – a laudable attempt to explain how large parts (or the whole) of an economy work, without pretending to know how the component parts work.

58

RALPH HARRIS, BARON HARRIS OF HIGH CROSS
1924–2006

SOURCE: *Growth, Advertising and the Consumer*
DATE: 1964
FIELD: Macroeconomics

Ralph Harris was a British economist who was appointed director-general of the Institute of Economic Affairs (IEA) in 1957—an organization set up a couple of years earlier in part as an antidote to the prevailing Keynesian economic orthodoxy of the age. Over the ensuing decades (he stayed with the IEA for more than 30 years), he became closely associated in the public mind with the Conservative Party—indeed, he had twice stood for election to parliament for the Conservatives in the early 1950s. However, after Prime Minister Margaret Thatcher made him a peer in the 1980s, he insisted on being a political independent in the House of Lords. But for all that, his economic affiliations were firmly with those who supported the primacy of the free market. In his time at the IEA, he developed relationships with other such notable free marketeer heavyweights as Friedrich Hayek and Milton Friedman.

However, as the wry quote here suggests, Harris acutely understood the dangers in believing one has all the answers to the big economic questions. His tongue-in-cheek definition of macroeconomics—a term coined by Ragnar Frisch in the early 1930s—acerbically reveals a fundamental truth: that each individual part of an economy could demand a lifetime's study, so that there is no realistic chance of being able to reliably predict the workings of the economy as a whole. Harris thus provided a chastening reminder for economists everywhere that they should not credit themselves with knowing it all. Nonetheless, as his own career evinced, he believed in the value of thinking around the subject as widely (and freely) as possible.

The labor movement
was the principal force
that transformed misery
and despair into hope
and progress.

59

MARTIN LUTHER KING, JR.
1929–1968

SOURCE: Address to the American Federation of Labor and Congress of Industrial Organizations
DATE: 1965
FIELD: Labor

Martin Luther King, Jr., was arguably the leading figure in the American civil rights movement in the 1960s. His doctrine of nonviolent civil disobedience and his sparkling oratory (honed over his career as a Southern Baptist minister) won him widespread admiration (he received the Nobel Peace Prize in 1964), even as his enemies increasingly feared his influence—an influence that endured far beyond his assassination in April 1968.

Though his reputation was built on his fight for the rights of America's black population, King recognized that a large component of the struggle was economic and that success might be more readily achieved by allying the black civil rights movement with the cause of the labor movement—a commitment that led to his critics regularly, and erroneously, branding him a communist. Referring to the labor movement in 1965, he said: "Out of its bold struggles, economic and social reform gave birth to unemployment insurance, old age pensions, government relief for the destitute, and above all new wage levels that meant not mere survival, but a tolerable life. The captains of industry did not lead this transformation; they resisted it until they were overcome."

He had identified the links between the two movements many years earlier. In 1961, for example, he observed: "Our needs are identical with labor's needs: decent wages, fair working conditions, livable housing, old-age security, health and welfare measures, conditions in which families can grow, have education for their children, and respect in the community. That is why Negroes support labor's demands...."

America's abundance was not created by public sacrifices to "the common good," but by the productive genius of free men who pursued their own personal interests.

60

AYN RAND
1905–1982

SOURCE: *Capitalism: The Unknown Ideal*
DATE: 1966
FIELD: Free markets

Russian-born Ayn Rand, who moved to the USA in her twenties, was a writer and philosopher who devised a philosophical system that she termed objectivism. Among its central tenets is the idea that the pursuit of individual happiness is a moral imperative. As she wrote in her 1938 novella *Anthem*: "I ask none to live for me, nor do I live for any others."

In economic terms, she favored laissez-faire capitalism as the model most capable of respecting and promoting the interests of the individual. It was a notion she investigated most fully in *Capitalism: The Unknown Ideal*. She believed that mutually beneficial human interactions result when "free men" are left to make "their own private fortunes." It was her contention that any attempt by the state to interfere in the economy represents an act of coercion that militates against the free use of reason—and by extension, stifles prolonged economic development and even the species' long-term survival, both of which she considered dependent on mankind's ability to reason free of the judgment or will of anyone else.

Rand countered the suggestion that her worldview represented a threat to social cohesion by arguing that by using reason, individuals realize their interests are best served by some degree of cooperation (for instance, by sharing out jobs according to abilities and skills). Government should thus be restricted to merely protecting the rights of the individual and, in economic terms, leaving everyone free to enter, or not, into any given transaction. While she dismissed the label herself, Rand is regarded by many as a champion of libertarianism in both the social and economic spheres.

Economic solutions create their own problems and move the economist relentlessly from one new frontier

to another.

61

WALTER W. HELLER
1915–1987

SOURCE: "What's Right with Economics?" in *American Economic Review*
DATE: 1975
FIELD: Macroeconomics

One of the leading economic figures in the postwar USA, Heller worked on the Marshall Plan that helped restore economic order to West Germany in the aftermath of conflict. But his profile was at its highest when he served as chairman of the Council of Economic Advisers in the administration first of President John F. Kennedy and then, briefly, of Lyndon Johnson.

A disciple of Keynes, Heller was instrumental in pushing the case for reducing rates of income tax—a move approved of by Kennedy and enacted under Johnson. At first sight, cutting taxes might seem contrary to the Keynesian preference for public spending, yet the move illustrates Heller's deep understanding of the complex mechanisms at play within the economy as a whole. As Kennedy would explain it to the Economic Club of New York in 1962, "It is a paradoxical truth that tax rates are too high today and tax revenues are too low and the soundest way to raise the revenues in the long run is to cut the rates now [...] And the reason is that only full employment can balance the budget, and tax reduction can pave the way to that employment."

Heller's article, "What's Right with Economics?" was a hardy defense of the job of the economist at a time, so he believed, when the prevailing fashion was to bash the profession. His quotation here expresses not negativity but a realistic acknowledgment that the business of economics is fraught with complexity—as one problem is solved, another presents itself. It is, he implied, the nature of the beast and should, perhaps, be embraced and not rejected.

I think the government solution to a problem is usually as bad as the problem and very often makes the problem worse.

62

MILTON FRIEDMAN

1912–2006

SOURCE: *An Economist's Protest*
DATE: 1975
FIELD: State intervention

Milton Friedman was arguably the single most influential economist in the second half of the 20th century. He was at the forefront of a broad rejection of Keynesianism from the 1950s onward, becoming the architect in chief of monetarism. Monetarism guided the economic policy of much of the developed world in the 1970s and 1980s, reaching its acme under Ronald Reagan in the USA and Margaret Thatcher in the UK.

Freidman rejected the Keynesian assertion that government spending could provide the short, sharp shot in the arm to reignite a failing economy. People spend (and so bolster the economy), Friedman argued, when they are confident in their long-term prospects. Expensive but short-lived government programs do not provide that security, he contended. Moreover, the sudden injection of money into the economy leads to inflation, which in turn results in higher wage demands, leading ultimately to companies laying off workers.

As was evidenced in several Western countries in the 1970s, it is possible to end up with the worst of all worlds: high inflation and high unemployment. Instead, Friedman suggested, governments best influence long-term economic health by controlling the money supply (ie, the volume of money printed and circulating) so that there is enough to meet consumer needs, and letting the markets deal with the problems of inflation and unemployment. In other words, governments should keep out of the economy as much as possible for fear of making things worse. Although his ideas have come under renewed scrutiny since the Great Recession, his economic philosophy remains highly influential.

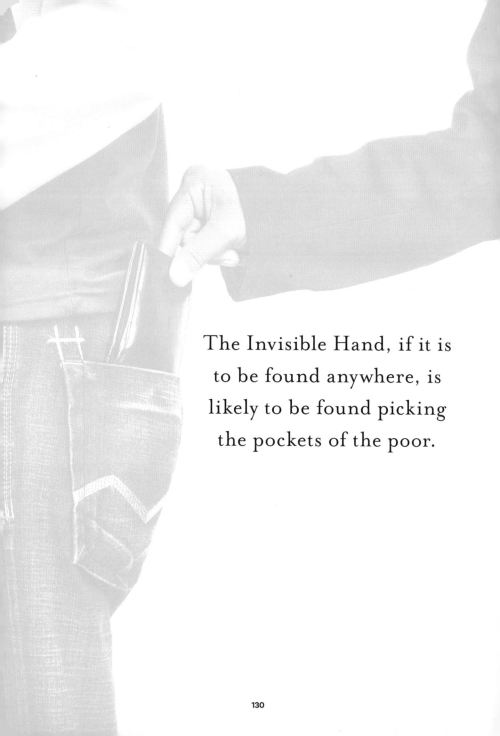

The Invisible Hand, if it is to be found anywhere, is likely to be found picking the pockets of the poor.

63

EDWARD J. NELL
b. 1935

SOURCE: "Value and Capital in Marxian Economics" in *The Crisis in Economic Theory*
DATE: 1981
FIELD: Free markets

Edward J. Nell is an economist who has spent much of his career at New York's New School for Social Research and has upheld that institution's reputation—established by the likes of one of its founders, Thorstein Veblen (see page 69) —for challenging established orthodoxies. He has developed, for instance, a General Theory of Transformational Growth that urges a new approach to economic analysis. Nell has suggested that the role of the markets, contrary to prevailing thought, should not be to allocate resources but rather to produce innovation that in turn forces changes to the way the markets work in an ongoing cycle of change and evolution.

A unifying theme of all his work has been a reconsideration of the traditional assumptions of the Neo-Classical school, which has promoted the superiority of free market systems. Where Neo-Classicists argue that the markets, for all their flaws, represent the best way to allocate resources, Nell is rather more skeptical. The Invisible Hand (a conceit originated by Adam Smith that the markets are compelled toward long-term equilibrium by an almost mystical force) is less concerned with bringing about equilibrium, Nell contends, than it is in enriching the wealthy at the expense of the poor in a race to establish market monopolies. As he put it in *Transformational Growth and Effective Demand* (1992): "Competition is a short-lived state of affairs; it is the race to get the monopoly—but it ends like the race between whales and minnows, with the winners swallowing the losers. The neo-Classical picture of 'the price mechanism efficiently allocating scarce resources' should be hung next to the round square in the Gallery of the Theatre of the Absurd."

The relative attractiveness of options varies when the same problem is framed in different ways.

The relative attractiveness of options varies when the same problem is framed in different ways.

64

DANIEL KAHNEMAN / AMOS TVERSKY
b. 1934 / b. 1937–1996

SOURCE: "The framing of decisions and the psychology of choice"
in *Science*
DATE: 1981
FIELD: Behavioral economics

Kahneman and Tversky had backgrounds in psychology, which they brought into the field of economics, ultimately earning a Nobel Prize. Their landmark observation that people make different choices depending on how the options are presented to them was at once both startling and entirely unsurprising. We all know that we may get a different answer depending on how we frame a particular question (Henry Ford famously observed that if he had asked people what they wanted, they would have said faster horses) but economists had been slow to integrate this knowledge. Kahneman and Tversky took on the task in their 1979 paper "Prospect Theory: An Analysis of Decisions Under Risk." In it, they undermined the classical view of consumers as risk-averse, risk-seeking, or risk-neutral, showing this depiction to be oversimplified and sometimes just wrong.

Instead, they proved that people are risk-loving when faced with the prospect of a loss but risk-averse when offered the chance of a gain. In other words, people are more loss-averse than gain-loving. Offer someone a guaranteed $100 or the 50 percent chance of being given $300, Kahneman and Tversky showed empirically, and most people opt for the safe $100. But reverse the question so that the choice is between an inevitable $100 loss or a 50 percent chance of a $300 loss, most who previously accepted the risk-averse $100 gain now chose the risk-seeking 50/50 chance of a $300 loss. The odds in each scenario were the same, but the framing of those odds prompted contradictory responses. This observation marked the death of the "rational consumer."

Trickle-down theory—
the less than elegant
metaphor that if one feeds
the horse enough oats,

some will pass through to
the road for the sparrows.

65

J. K. GALBRAITH
1908–2006

SOURCE: "Recession Economics" in *The New York Review of Books*
DATE: 1982
FIELD: Trickle-down economics

A leading liberal voice in the American landscape of the second half of the 20th century, Galbraith recognized the role of the markets in increasing overall prosperity but also espoused elements of Keynesianism. In his most famous work, *The Affluent Society* (1958), he highlighted how the nation's public sector was lagging behind the growth of the private sector and urged public spending on infrastructure to address growing wealth inequality. By the time he wrote "Recession Economics" in the 1980s, he was increasingly concerned that the wealthy of the developed world had grown complacent while the poor were having their routes out of poverty restricted in an unprecedented way. He saved particular criticism for trickle-down theory—the idea that tax breaks and other benefits for big business and the rich are good for all because they promote economic growth, creating new jobs, and raising wages for those at the bottom of the economic pile.

While Galbraith accepted that some of the benefit may pass through (the undigested oats, as it were), this was little more than the detritus. The theory requires, he said, belief that business executives, because of their tax bracket, are idling away their time but tax reductions will put them back to work. "I have a far better view of the American businessman," he said. "I judge him to be working very hard now, and I believe him to be decently ensconced in the American dream. Given more money, and with the help of his wife and family, he will spend and enjoy most of it."

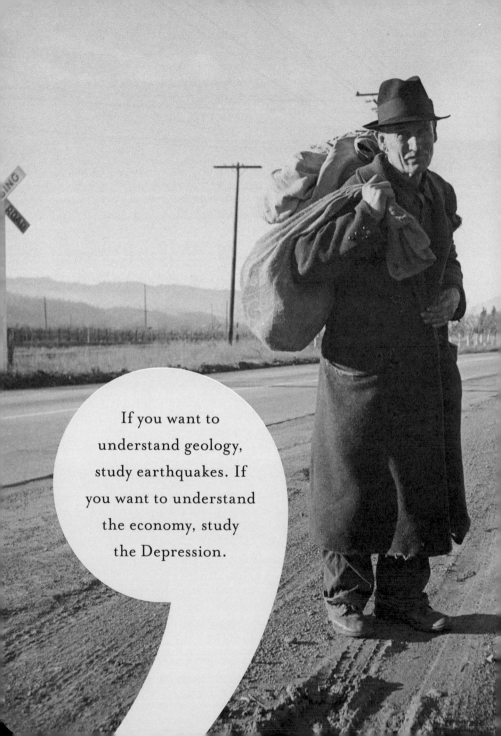

If you want to understand geology, study earthquakes. If you want to understand the economy, study the Depression.

66

BEN BERNANKE
b. 1953

SOURCE: *The Wall Street Journal*
DATE: 1983
FIELD: Economic cycles

Ben Bernanke was chairman of the Federal Reserve when economic crisis hit the USA and quickly spread around the world in 2007. By then, his interest in the Great Depression of the 1930s was near legendary, although few foresaw that he would be at the forefront of dealing with the country's biggest economic crisis since those grim days. In the period 1929 to 1933, US output decreased by almost a third, the unemployment rate stood at 25 percent, and thousands of banks went to the wall. Individuals and businesses struggled to meet their debt commitments, and the standard of living for millions of people collapsed.

As the extent of the financial crisis of 2007 became evident, Bernanke found himself with the responsibility of leading the country away from a similar meltdown. He had concluded that a slow response to events by the authorities in the 1930s, allied to unfettered panic in the banking sector, had turned the Wall Street Crash into an unparalleled disaster. So, Bernanke coordinated a rapid national—and international—response to the 2007 crisis, including bringing down interest rates to 0 percent and backing a hugely expensive initiative known as Quantitative Easing that saw governments provide banks with cash in order to maintain liquidity. Though the effectiveness of Bernanke's response remains a subject of much debate, he is convinced that, thanks to quick action and unorthodox strategies, the Great Recession did not wreak quite the same havoc on so many lives as the Great Depression.

We have a new kind of bank.
It is called too big to fail.

67

STEWART BRETT MCKINNEY

1931–1987

SOURCE: *Report of Congressional Inquiry into Continental Illinois National Bank*
DATE: 1984
FIELD: Banking

Until the banking crisis of 2007–2008, the 1984 collapse of the Continental Illinois National Bank and Trust Company (once the seventh-largest commercial bank in the USA) was that country's largest ever bank failure. The response of the authorities was to bring it under the management of the Federal Deposit Insurance Corporation. In the subsequent Congressional hearings into the affair, it was McKinney—the member of the House of Representatives for Connecticut's 4th congressional district—who brought the term "too big to fail" into popular usage. His words acknowledged the existence of financial institutions that are considered so large and so vital to the health of the wider financial system that governments choose to intervene and prop them up when they fail, rather than let them go to the wall.

The concept came under renewed scrutiny in 2007 and 2008 when a large number of international financial institutions were bailed out from the public purse. For many economists, the phenomenon sits uncomfortably. For one thing, it seems like a perversion of the free-market ideals most banks advocate. The market, after all, demands that those actors unable to create a self-sustaining model give way to competition. Then there is the problem of moral hazard—that is to say, the principle that institutions will act recklessly in pursuit of profit in the knowledge that they will not be allowed to go under. As Alan Greenspan, chairman of the Federal Reserve from 1987 to 2006, put it in 2009: "If they're too big to fail, they're too big."

Men won't easily give up
a system in which half the
world's population works
for next to nothing.

68

MARILYN WARING
b. 1952

SOURCE: *The Guardian*
DATE: 1989
FIELD: Feminist economics

An academic who in 1975 won a seat in New Zealand's parliament (she was the youngest member in the country at the time), Marilyn Waring is probably best known for her landmark economic study, *If Women Counted*, published in 1988. With systematic rigor, she launched an attack on the way in which much economic orthodoxy has overlooked the contribution made to economic well-being by women. So, for instance, she sought to illustrate how Gross Domestic Product—the internationally accepted measure of a country's overall economic productivity over a specific time period—skews data in favor of men.

Waring pointed out that much vital work upon which economies ultimately rely—from running households to bringing up children and looking after the sick and elderly—have been traditionally undertaken by women without any formal record being kept. Without childcare, there would be no future reliable workforce, while caring for relatives saves the state vast sums it might otherwise have to spend on contracted care provision. Business, as well, has been impacted by that fact that women traditionally ensured a comfortable domestic setting to which the "Captains of Industry"—largely male—could return to recharge their batteries.

Yet all of these contributions have been treated as virtually invisible for most of history. While the work of a cleaner in a hotel or a worker in a hospital is recorded in a nation's GDP, the comparable efforts of a wife, mother, or carer in the domestic setting are ignored. Waring suggested this was less an error of omission than a tool of the patriarchy to devalue the traditional work sphere of women so that it need not be paid for.

They talk about
the failure of socialism
but where is the success of
capitalism in Africa, Asia,
and Latin America?

69

1926–2016

SOURCE: Public statement following the collapse of the USSR
DATE: 1991
FIELDS: Socialism, communism

Fidel Castro was the communist revolutionary who overthrew the government of Fulgencio Batista in 1959 and subsequently ran Cuba as a one-party communist state for almost half a century. Although a relatively small island nation, its proximity to the USA ensured that Cuba punched above its weight as a player in international affairs. Domestically, though, Cuba struggled to maintain itself economically. The collapse of the Soviet Union, which had provided economic and strategic support, ushered in a decade of serious decline, characterized by food and energy shortages.

Yet Castro, in common with a great many of the leading Marxist-communist leaders of the 20th century, remained committed to his agenda. As he explained at the time of the Soviet dissolution: "Among other things, we cannot forget that 1.2 billion people live in China under socialism. The Chinese people suffered from misery and hunger for thousands of years, and only socialism could perform the miracle of freeing that country where only 100 million hectares sustain 1.1 billion people."

Castro claimed that capitalism had, by contrast, caused poverty, hunger, backwardness, and underdevelopment for millions. "Where is the success of capitalism in places where thousands of millions of people live? […] Capitalism failed in more than 100 countries, which now face a truly desperate situation." Certainly, capitalism has endured its challenges in the decades since Castro spoke these words, while Cuba has persevered among a diminishing number of communist states. For how much longer, though, is not clear.

The greater the inequality [...]

the lower growth.

70

ALBERTO ALESINA / DANI RODRIK
b. 1957 / b. 1957

SOURCE: "Distributive Politics and Economic Growth" in *The Quarterly Journal of Economics*
DATE: 1994
FIELD: Growth

Alberto Alesina, Italian, and Dani Rodrik, Turkish, worked on the question of the relationship between wealth distribution and economic growth in part as a response to the work of Russian-American economist Simon Kuznets. In the 1950s and 1960s Kuznets had devised the "Kuznets Curve," which sought to trace the impact of industrial growth on per capita income. He broadly concluded that as an economy moves from an agricultural to an industrial base (a traditional step in the process of economic development), per capita income rises but with the greater proportion accruing to those who already hold capital and can take advantage of investment opportunities. A surge of workers from the countryside to the cities meanwhile keeps wages low for most people.

Nonetheless, Kuznets found, over the long term, wages stabilize and the higher levels of education and welfare that tend to accompany urbanization and industrialization lead to a decline in inequality. Alesina and Rodrik took a different approach. Rather than how growth affects inequality, they looked at the question the other way around—how inequality affects growth. Their stark conclusion was that more equal societies grow more quickly, since societies with greater wealth disparity tend toward a higher tax rate on accumulated wealth (to satisfy the less wealthy majority), which acts as a disincentive to further economic expansion. As they put it: "A crude distinction between economics and politics would be that economics is concerned with expanding the pie while politics is about distributing it [...] Our main conclusion is that inequality is conducive to the adoption of growth-retarding policies."

You try to be greedy
when others are fearful.
And you try to be fearful
when others are greedy.

71

WARREN BUFFETT

b. 1930

SOURCE: *Buffett: The Making of an American Capitalist*
by Roger Lowenstein
DATE: 1995
FIELD: Investing

Warren Buffett, the chief executive officer of holding company Berkshire Hathaway, has an almost legendary reputation as an investor, having won himself a fortune approaching $90 billion as of 2018. As such, he has become an iconic figure to millions of aspiring investors across the globe. As well as a magnate and speculator, he is also known as one of the world's foremost philanthropists. Along with Microsoft founder Bill Gates and Facebook boss Mark Zuckerberg, in 2009 he established the Giving Pledge, which encourages billionaires to give away at least half of their fortunes to good causes.

According to Buffett, the words quoted opposite represent the "secret to getting rich on Wall Street." Central to his success has been an ability to identify stocks that are fundamentally undervalued—often, stocks that have intrinsic long-term value but which are facing some short-term crisis. This allows him to buy at a low price and sell later at a higher one, when the stock's value has restored its equilibrium, or alternatively to buy into companies for the long haul in the expectation of strong future returns. In other words, he attempts to steer clear of the herd mentality that can lead to erroneous short-term judgments as to a company's worth—both in terms of undervaluation and overvaluation.

Always a calm head, his ability to analyze a company's health from its numbers and not from the gossip that surrounds it has ensured him unimaginable wealth. As he famously put it: "In the short term the market is a popularity contest; in the long term it is a weighing machine."

Economic things matter only in so far as they make people happier.

72

ANDREW J. OSWALD
b. 1953

SOURCE: "Happiness and Economic Performance" in *The Economic Journal*
DATE: 1997
FIELD: Performance

Oswald, who has held senior academic posts at elite universities throughout the world, has been a trailblazer in the area of happiness economics—a field that has garnered increasing attention since the latter part of the 20th century. While economics has for most of its history dealt in quantitative analysis—as in measuring a nation's economic health by studying the progress of its Gross Domestic Product—happiness economics is more interested in qualitative analysis. Encompassing aspects of psychology, sociology, and health, it examines the relationships between economic conditions and overall happiness. Although it is necessarily subjective, it nevertheless seeks to model levels of happiness in as scientific a way as possible, for instance by accumulating data from surveys.

At its heart is the idea that traditional measures of economic success are redundant in the absence of increasing general levels of happiness. The data often throws up surprising conclusions. In Oswald's words: "If a nation's economic performance improves, how much extra happiness does that buy its citizens? Most public debate assumes—without real evidence—that the answer is a lot [...] In industrialized countries, well-being appears to rise as real national income grows. But the rise is so small as to be sometimes almost undetectable." Unemployment, however, he noted, appears to be a major source of unhappiness, suggesting that governments ought to try to reduce the amount of joblessness. His conclusion, then, was: "In a country that is already rich, policy aimed instead at raising economic growth may be of comparatively little value."

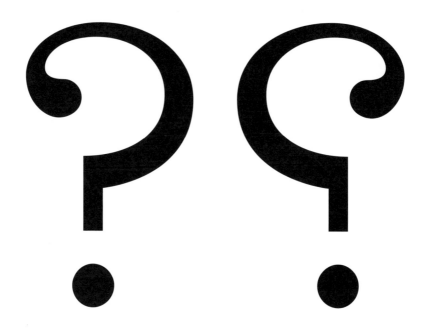

Economics is a choice
between alternatives
all the time. Those
are the trade-offs.

73

PAUL SAMUELSON
1915–2009

SOURCE: PBS NewsHour
DATE: 1999
FIELD: Opportunity cost

Paul Samuelson was the first American winner of the Nobel Prize for Economics, his citation stating that he had "done more than any other contemporary economist to raise the level of scientific analysis in economic theory."

In the quotation opposite—one which echoes the ideas of Lionel Robbins (see page 91)—he suggested economics is at one level simply a question of opportunity cost. Samuelson gave the example of a lawyer who's the best typist in town—better even than his own secretary. "But he would be crazy to be typing up his legal briefs because he's displacing billable time," Samuelson observed, "$100 an hour, to be doing what is paid about $12 an hour, at best." He concluded that time is our ultimate scarce resource and so we are continually forced to sacrifice alternative activities to get the one that pleases us most. That is why, he suggested, we should all be economists, considering what we are giving up at every turn in order to establish a pattern that gives us the best chance of making choices that bring us most happiness.

However, he warned against becoming too embroiled in the process. "Seeking for the very, very best meal in life is a miserable existence," he said. "What you want is what Herbert Simon, the great Carnegie Tech psychologist/economist, says is to 'satisfice'—get a good sustainable solution. That's better than seeking endlessly for the very best [...] Be thoughtful, don't be in denial, but don't sweat it beyond that."

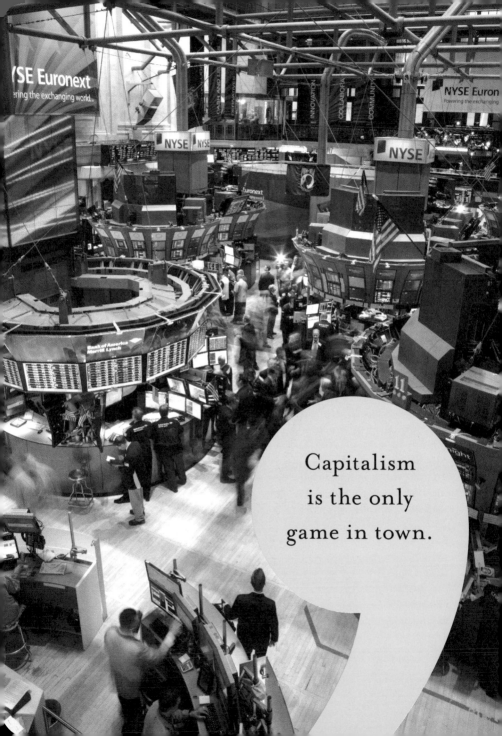

Capitalism is the only game in town.

74

HERNANDO DE SOTO
b. 1941

SOURCE: *The Mystery of Capital*
DATE: 2000
FIELD: Capitalism

A Peruvian economist, Hernando de Soto is known for his studies of informal economies and how they impact economic growth. He has long argued that the lack of formal property rights holds back many emerging economies. Where informal sectors play a disproportionately large role in a nation's economy, he argues, the unreported nature of transactions and the lack of legally recognized ownership traps people into an endless informal cycle. Individuals are unable to access credit (as they lack proof of their assets), so cannot grow their businesses or engage in the legal system to settle disputes.

In short, individuals trapped in informal economies are unable to convert their labor into capital. "Capitalism stands alone as the only feasible way to rationally organize a modern economy," de Soto has said. "At this moment in history, no responsible nation has a choice [...] I am not a die-hard capitalist. I do not view capitalism as a credo. Much more important to me are freedom, compassion for the poor, respect for the social contract, and equal opportunity. But for the moment, to achieve those goals, capitalism is the only game in town. It is the only system we know that provides us with the tools required to create massive surplus value."

By establishing the legal frameworks to allow more people to prove legal title to property, he contends, individuals are suddenly able to make contracts with strangers, so vastly expanding markets and increasing the chance of long-term prosperity across the economy as a whole.

I believe that virtually all the problems in the world come from inequality

of one kind

or another.

75

AMARTYA SEN
b. 1933

SOURCE: *The Progressive*
DATE: 2001
FIELD: Inequality

Amartya Sen, awarded the 1998 economics Nobel Prize "for his contributions to welfare economics," has argued that—while he believes in many aspects of the market economy—the failure of the global economy to allocate resources in an equitable manner is at the root of most crises.

In his 1981 paper, "Poverty and Famines: An Essay on Entitlement and Deprivation," Sen contended that the devastating Bengal famine of 1943—which cost some three million lives—along with several subsequent famines in Africa and Asia, resulted not from an absolute lack of food, but an inability to get food to those in need. He pointed out that in Bengal that year, food production was actually higher than it had been in previous, famine-free years. However, a surge of money from the UK into the Indian wartime economy was centered on the imperial capital, Calcutta, causing price inflation. Poorly paid rural workers and the urban poor were unable to access basic goods and services (or "entitlements," as Sen calls them). The food was there but millions lacked the financial resources to access it. The failure of crops, Sen suggested, was less damaging than the failure of allocation.

However, Sen remains hopeful that such problems may be addressed in our interconnected world by ensuring strong oversight. "Globalization can be very unjust and unfair and unequal," he said in 2001, "but these are matters under our control. It's not that we don't need the market economy. We need it. But the market economy should not have priority or dominance over other institutions."

People need to invest in themselves
during their whole lives.

76

1930–2014

SOURCE: "The Age of Human Capital" in *Education in the Twenty-First Century* (ed. Edward P. Lazear)
DATE: 2002
FIELD: Human capital

Gary Becker, once described by the *New York Times* as "the most important social scientist in the past 50 years," was a leading exponent of behavioral economics. The 1992 Nobel Prize-winner worked across an array of fields, applying microeconomic analyses to, for example, crime, family life, and employment. One of his most celebrated works was *Human Capital* (1964), which investigated how an individual's knowledge, skills, behavior, personality, and so on may produce economic value.

While some found such "commodification" of human beings distasteful, Becker's compelling argument stated that human capital may be seen as a "means of production." Writing in 2002, he said that human capital has grown in significance since the 1980s and is crucial to the international division of labor. Moreover, investment in it customarily leads to increased output—and, by extension, greater rewards for the individual. And of all the possible investments in human capital, none is more important than education. Yet, as he pointed out, much learning goes unmeasured by companies and adults outside the formal education system, despite its crucial contribution to stimulating innovation.

Becker also predicted that distance learning would take on an increasingly vital role in the global economy. Perhaps most significantly for the individual, he believed that lifelong training and education is vital to maximizing one's economic potential. To put it another way, to keep on learning is the greatest investment you can make in yourself.

The reason that the invisible hand often seems invisible is that it is often not there.

77

JOSEPH STIGLITZ
b. 1943

SOURCE: *The Guardian*
DATE: 2002
FIELD: Free markets

Joseph Stiglitz, a Nobel Prize-winning former chief economist of the World Bank and chairman of the presidential Council of Economic Advisers, has cautioned against being in thrall to the excesses of laissez-faire economics—what he referred to as "market fundamentalism."

In the article from which the quotation opposite is taken, Stiglitz argued that central tenets of "market fundamentalism" were unsound. For instance, he said, participants in economic transactions do not all have access to the same information when making decisions, nor do they act with perfect rationality, nor are markets perfectly efficient. Adam Smith's fabled "invisible hand" is, he suggested, an illusion. He emphasized instead "how important it is to study people and economies as they are, not as we want them to be. Only by understanding better actual human behavior can we hope to design policies that will make our economies work better as well."

In particular, Stiglitz doubts the ability of markets to function properly where there are externalities—those consequences of commercial actions for which the responsible party is neither charged nor compensated. As he told the *International Herald Tribune* in 2006: "Markets, by themselves, produce too much pollution. Markets, by themselves, also produce too little basic research [...] But recent research has shown that these externalities are pervasive, whenever there is imperfect information or imperfect risk markets—that is always. Government plays an important role in banking and securities regulation, and [...] some regulation is required to make markets work [...] The real debate today is about finding the right balance between the market and government."

The blunt truth about the politics of climate change is that no country will want to sacrifice its economy in order to meet this challenge.

78

TONY BLAIR
b. 1953

SOURCE: *The Guardian*
DATE: 2005
FIELD: Environmental economics

In a speech of 2004 Tony Blair, the United Kingdom's prime minister from 1997 until 2007, called climate change "the world's greatest environmental challenge." "What is now plain," he said, "is that the emission of greenhouse gases, associated with industrialization and strong economic growth from a world population that has increased sixfold in 200 years, is causing global warming at a rate that began as significant, has become alarming and is simply unsustainable in the longterm."

Yet just a year later Blair was accused of back-pedaling and undermining international efforts to reduce greenhouse emissions. He claimed that legally binding targets had the effect of making economic actors nervous: "People fear some external force is going to impose some internal target on you [...] to restrict your economic growth." Even as his critics accused him of a failure of nerve, there was plentiful evidence to back up his concerns. The USA was the most notable nonsignatory of the 1992 Kyoto Protocol on the grounds that putting a cap on its pollution would damage its economy. There was also objection to the target exemptions extended to rapidly industrializing nations such as India and China. And in 2012 Canada withdrew from the agreement, in part because it feared large penalties for failure to reach its targets.

Though most environmentalists are adamant that the real economic cost will come from a collective failure to address climate change—leading to greater frequency of extreme weather incidents, rising sea levels, lower crop yields, declining health—striking a balance with shorter-term economic and political considerations poses an ongoing challenge.

A pension
is nothing more
than deferred
compensation.

79

ELIZABETH WARREN

b. 1949

SOURCE: PBS Frontline
DATE: 2006
FIELD: Pensions

Elizabeth Warren, a US senator who previously taught at Harvard Law School, is well known for her consumer protection campaigns. In 2006 she spoke out against the trend for companies in financial difficulty to use legal means (including bankruptcy legislation) to abandon their pension commitments. Referring to pensions as "deferred compensation," she explained, "It's an employer who says, in effect, 'I'll pay you $1,000, but $800 of it you'll get in a pay check today, and the other $200, I'm going to hang on to it on your behalf and put it aside, and these are the promises I'll make for when you retire.'"

Warren's words are particularly pertinent in view of the pensions time-bomb that most developed economies face. With rapidly aging populations, low ratios of workers to retirees, and insufficient resources set aside, the elevated levels of pension enjoyed by successive generations are unlikely to be available in the future. In the USA, for example, the extent of unfunded pension obligations is measured in trillions of dollars.

However, Warren warned against companies rashly restructuring their commitments. "When all of those individual workers, when those tens of thousands, hundreds of thousands, millions of people don't have the money they were counting on, instead of having an economy that grows, we have an economy that starts to shrink," she said. "And then comes the psychological effect [...] the people who are just scared: 'I've got a job today, but do I know it's going to be there tomorrow? And what about that pension? I'm 15 years away from retirement—will it really be there?'"

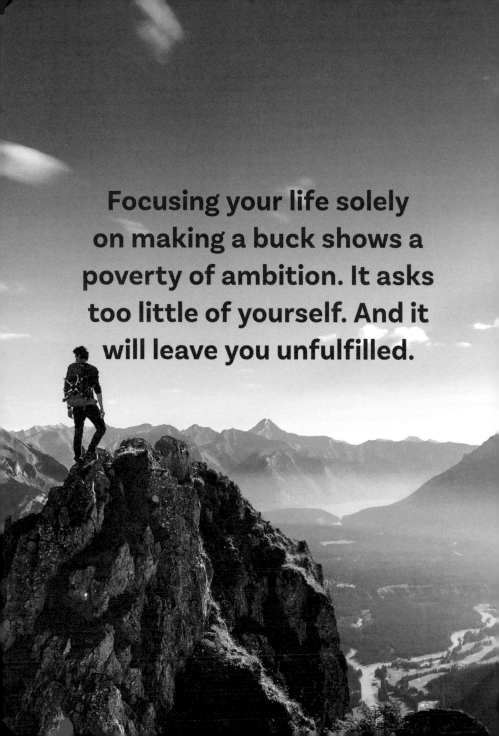

Focusing your life solely on making a buck shows a poverty of ambition. It asks too little of yourself. And it will leave you unfulfilled.

80

BARACK OBAMA
b. 1961

SOURCE: Speech at Campus Progress Annual Conference
DATE: 2006
FIELD: Materialism

At a time when Barack Obama was starting to make waves in the American political firmament but few were predicting his ascent to the White House, he spoke repeatedly of his wish that people focus less on the material trappings of wealth and more on maximizing their potential as human beings. Though such words might have sounded gauche from the mouth of someone born to wealth and power, from Obama they carried a certain moral authority. Although his childhood was not marked out by poverty, he overcame great obstacles—not least the prejudice he faced for being mixed-race. His decision to pursue a career in politics came with no guarantee of either success or riches.

So there was weight to his words as he told an audience of new graduates in 2006: "It's very easy to just take that diploma, forget about all this progressive politics stuff, and go chasing after the big house and the large salary and the nice suits and all the other things that our money culture says you should buy. But I hope you don't."

As it transpired, Obama would see out his presidency under the shadow of the Great Recession, when the lofty material aspirations of many gave way to a more basic hope that they could meet their mortgage repayments and other rudimentary financial obligations. Nonetheless, Obama continued to emphasize that there really is more to life than money. As he told *Vanity Fair* in 2016, he still longs for "a world in which every kid, regardless of their background, can strive and achieve and fulfill their potential."

The people in debt become hopeless, and the hopeless people don't vote.

81

TONY BENN

1925–2014

SOURCE: Interview in Michael Moore's *Sicko*
DATE: 2007
FIELD: Political economy

The relationship between voting patterns and economic conditions has long been a source of fascination to politicians and pundits alike. Nonetheless, drawing concrete conclusions about how one impacts the other has proved problematic. Statistics indicate, however, that in many democratic nations the poorest individuals are less likely to exercise their right to vote. In the UK general election of 2010, for instance, there was a gap of 23 percentage points between the turnout of the richest and poorest income groups. Similarly, in the 2012 US presidential election, the participation rate among those living in households earning less than $20,000 was below 50 percent but stood at 77 percent for those in households with incomes of more than $75,000.

Benn, regarded as a stalwart of the Left in UK politics during his almost half-century as a member of parliament, was adamant that the reason poor people are less inclined to vote is because they have little hope that any candidate can resolve their problems. As he put it: "Choice depends on the freedom to choose and if you are shackled with debt you don't have the freedom to choose." Poverty and indebtedness pose, he suggested, a threat to democratic ideals.

James Carville, Bill Clinton's campaign strategist during the 1992 presidential campaign, saw things differently. It was his contention that electoral success was dependent upon selling a message of credible economic hope. Persuade those in economic difficulties that you can make things better, and electoral success is yours. That was the implication of his now immortal words as to what Clinton's campaign workers should focus on: "The economy, stupid."

This is our greatest challenge: learning to live in a crowded and interconnected world that is creating unprecedented pressures on human society and on the physical environment

82

JEFFREY SACHS

b. 1954

SOURCE: BBC Reith Lectures
DATE: 2007
FIELD: Globalization

Jeffrey Sachs, a world authority on sustainable development, used the Reith Lectures to outline the many challenges faced by our "extraordinarily crowded world." "It's bursting at the seams," he said, "in human terms, in economic terms, and in ecological terms." Warning that we have so far failed to heed the seriousness of the problems we confront, he argued that an equitable economic system—and one that doesn't wreck the environment—is crucial to achieving peace and human happiness.

Sachs highlighted how the speedy diffusion of technological developments offers "the fabulous prospect for the rapid closing of economic gaps that now exist between the rich and the poor"—in turn causing a fundamental shift in the global balance of economic and political power, as evidenced by the rise of India and China. Nonetheless, he said, a billion people on the planet remain too hungry, poor, burdened by disease, and stripped of the most basic infrastructure to make the first vital steps on to the development ladder.

Sachs urged the richest countries of the world to rise to this challenge not merely with words but with actions too—something that hitherto the developed world has been reluctant to do at the required level. "The rich world seems to believe," he said, "[...] that this doesn't really matter, because the actions of the rich countries don't begin to address this problem. We are leaving ten million people to die every year because they are too poor to stay alive. Fine speeches will not solve that problem."

We are in the midst of a once-in-a-century credit tsunami.

83

ALAN GREENSPAN

b. 1926

SOURCE: House of Representatives' Oversight and Reform Committee
DATE: 2008
FIELD: Economic crises

Greenspan, who served as Chairman of the US Federal Reserve between 1987 and 2006, spoke these words to a government committee investigating how the great credit crisis of 2007 had come about. During his time with the Fed, Greenspan became known as a passionate defender of the free market. As such, he was reluctant to interfere in the workings of the mortgage market, from which emerged the housing bubble that burst so disastrously in 2007. Greenspan would subsequently tell the House Committee that he did "not understand exactly how it [the crisis] happened" but predicted that chastened investors would be exceptionally cautious and that the markets "will be far more restrained than would any currently contemplated new regulatory regime."

Greenspan also took to the media to address allegations that he ought to have done more to avert the crisis—a view put forward by the committee chairman, Henry Waxman, who said that the disaster might have been prevented "if regulators had paid more attention and intervened with responsible legislation. The list of regulatory mistakes and misjudgments is long and the cost to taxpayers and the economy is staggering."

Writing in the *Financial Times*, Greenspan went on record to defend his actions. "My view of the range of dispersion of outcomes has been shaken," he wrote, "but not my judgment that free competitive markets are by far the unrivalled way to organize economies [...] We have tried regulation ranging from heavy to central planning. None meaningfully worked. Do we wish to retest the evidence?"

Why did no one see it coming?

84

QUEEN ELIZABETH II
b. 1926

SOURCE: Said during visit to the London School of Economics
DATE: 2008
FIELD: Forecasting

Queen Elizabeth II has spent much of her career avoiding explicitly political questions. However, in 2008 she voiced the thoughts of many ordinary people as they wrestled with the impacts of the global economic crisis: Why had the world's economic experts failed to see what was around the corner? There was a sense that economic forecasters had fallen foul of an epidemic of complacency, whose roots may be traced to the collapse of Soviet communism in the early 1990s.

Political economist Francis Fukuyama suggested at that time that we had reached "the end of history." The Western liberal capitalist model had prevailed and there was no holding it back—an opinion consolidated by several years of robust growth throughout the developed world. No one wanted to call time on this particular party. But by 2007 the cracks were beginning to show, starting in the US housing sector. Mortgage companies had loaned money to individuals who couldn't afford to pay it back. At the same time, financial institutions found themselves dangerously exposed to bad loans after years of dealing in increasingly complex (and little understood) financial products.

When the entire edifice began to collapse, it took a raft of banks and investors with it. Of course, there had been a few dissenting voices—Peter Schiff and Nouriel Roubini notably gained fame for having warned of impending catastrophe. But the episode damaged the reputation of economic forecasters incalculably. As a group of leading British economists put it in 2009, there had been a "failure of the collective imagination."

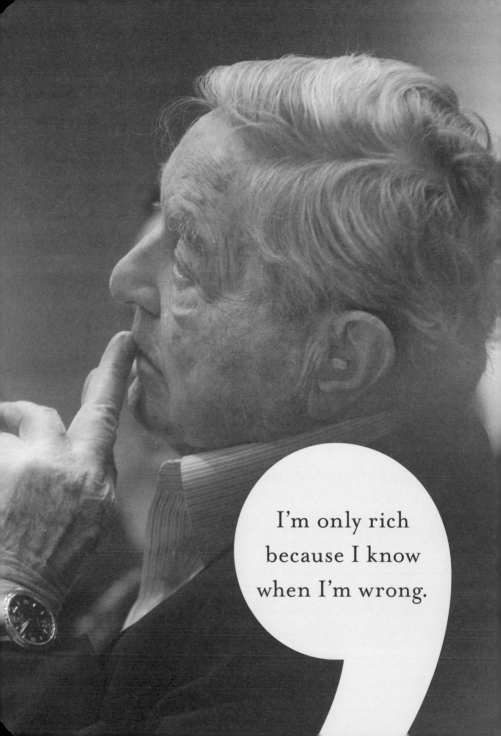

85

GEORGE SOROS
b. 1930

SOURCE: *Wall Street Journal*
DATE: 2008
FIELD: Investing

Soros, born in Hungary into a Jewish family, survived the Nazi occupation of that country before moving to the UK in 1947 to study at the London School of Economics. He subsequently went to the USA to work firstly in banking and then to run his own hedge funds. He shot to public attention in 1992 when he bet against the pound during a day-long currency crisis known as Black Wednesday, earning himself around $1 billion in the process. He was highly influenced by the scientific philosophy of Karl Popper, who argued that empirical evidence can never be known with absolute certainty. It must be verified by repeated testing, Popper said, and may at any stage be undermined by a negative result.

Soros developed this idea into his own theory of reflexivity, with special reference to its impacts on the market. Soros sees a yawning gap between the certainties that economists traditionally assume (such as the notion of market equilibrium and the idea of the rational economic actor) and the many personal biases and gaps in knowledge that impact real-life economic interactions. As such, he is alert to anomalies in market behavior and quick to respond when his own assumptions are shown to be incorrect. This conceptual framework, he has said, allows him to better explain and predict events than most others. With a fortune measured in billions of dollars, Soros has reaped the rewards of accepting that the markets are subject not to a set of fixed rules but to the vagaries of human behavior. As he put it to the *Wall Street Journal*: "I basically have survived by recognizing my mistakes."

Africa is addicted to aid.

86

DAMBISA MOYO
b. 1969

SOURCE: *Dead Aid: Why Aid Is Not Working and How There Is a Better Way for Africa*
DATE: 2009
FIELD: International aid

Zambian-born Moyo caused ripples with the publication of *Dead Aid*, in which she attempted to show how current models of international aid—that is to say, the transfer of resources from one (usually richer) country to another—have contributed to holding back economic development across Africa. Moyo is not the first to debate the benefits, or lack thereof, derived from international aid. In general, aid comes in one of two forms—emergency aid, to alleviate suffering caused by a specific incident such as famine, and development aid that seeks to encourage longer-term economic growth.

Since 1970, the United Nations has recommended a target of 0.7 percent of donor nation's national incomes. Moyo, though, claims that the billions of dollars given by rich Western nations to poor African ones encourage a culture of aid dependency and discourage genuine economic development. Aid, she suggests, encourages rent-seeking behavior and corrupt government (as individuals or organizations attempt to divert funds in a nontransparent way), while failing to promote good oversight and the development of those strong institutions vital to a prosperous, open economy. In some instances, she says, aid has prolonged wars, as opposing groups look to siphon off funding.

Moyo's critics claim her arguments play into the hands of those opposed to international aid on the basis of cost. Nonetheless, she holds that the time is ripe for a different approach—one that will see the breaking of the aid cycle in favor of, among other things, supporting the strengthening of property rights, providing greater access to credit, and increasing foreign direct investment.

The customer
has always driven the
business model.

87

AMANCIO ORTEGA
b. 1936

SOURCE: Inditex Annual Report
DATE: 2009
FIELD: Consumerism

The world's wealthiest retailer with a fortune of more than $66 billion in 2018, Ortega is the founder of the Zara chain of fashion shops and former chairman of the Inditex retail group. At the heart of his business philosophy has been the idea that everything begins and ends with the customer. As he would reiterate in the Inditex annual report of 2010: "The customer must continue to be our main center of attention, both in the creation of our fashion collections and in the design of our shops, of our logistical system and of any other activity."

Ortega was, thus, less worried about stocking his shops in response to what his rivals were doing or what was seen on the fashion catwalks of New York, Paris, and Milan than in keeping track of what was being said by his customers and across the myriad fashion bloggers on the Internet.

To this extent, Ortega found himself in the company of Amazon founder Jeff Bezos, who in 2015 observed: "Many companies describe themselves as customer-focused, but few walk the walk. Most big technology companies are competitor-focused. They see what others are doing, and then work to follow fast." Of course, Ortega was by no means the first major retailer to privilege the customer above all else—Harry Gordon Selfridge, the famous department store magnate, was among those who claimed that "The customer is always right"—but few have lived by the credo with such dedication and success as Ortega.

Ecological economics
recognizes that the economy,
like any other subsystem on the
planet, cannot grow forever.

88

ROBERT COSTANZA

b. 1950

SOURCE: *Yale Insights*
DATE: 2010
FIELD: Ecological economics

Costanza has been at the forefront of the ecological school of economics since the 1990s. Ecological economics, he has said, is neither a subdiscipline of economics or ecology, but rather a bridge between the two that also encompasses aspects of psychology, anthropology, archaeology, and history. To that extent, it is a field that seeks to create an integrated picture of human interaction in the past, now and into the future. It strives to understand how we, as individuals and societies, operate as economic agents within our wider ecological support system, in the hope of outlining routes to a sustainable future. Costanza sees it as separate from the field of environmental economics, which he considers applies mainstream economic thinking to the environment—for instance, accepting the preeminence of the markets and striving to deal with the problem of externalities (see page 77) like pollution.

By contrast, ecological economics, he says, "tries to study everything outside the market as well as everything inside the market and bring the two together." Conventional economics, he contends, doesn't generally recognize questions of scale—"the fact that we live on a finite planet, or that the economy, as a subsystem, cannot grow indefinitely into this larger, containing system." Instead, the mainstream view thinks that technology can solve any and all problems related to finite resources. Costanza's view is, however, very different: "It's not that we can't continue to improve the human situation. But we have to recognize that the environment creates certain limits and constraints on that, and we can define a safe operating space within which we can do the best we can."

The Occupy Wall Street protests at last suggest that America's wealth gap is once again becoming an organizing political principle in the country.

89

JON MEACHAM
b. 1969

SOURCE: *Time*
DATE: 2011
FIELD: Political economy

Jon Meacham, an American historian, editor, and author, wrote in 2011 of his
hope that economic populism—as epitomized by the "Occupy" movement—
might become a significant force within the political scene. The movement
began with the Occupy Wall Street (OWS) protest in September 2011 against
social and economic inequality in all its forms. OWS adopted the slogan "We
are the 99 percent," referencing the disparity between the wealth levels of the
US's richest 1 percent and everybody else.

The movement quickly spread to other venues throughout the city, the country,
and internationally. In its growth, Meacham saw a return to an earlier mode of
protest. "From the 1820s to the 1960s," he said, "the major engine of the
politics of the few versus the many was more about money and power than it
was about symbols and power. From Andrew Jackson to William Jennings
Bryan to Harry Truman, leaders rallied in support of 'the little guy who has no
pull,' in Truman's phrase."

However, according to Meacham, since the mid-1960s the conversation had
moved from economics to culture—toward targets such as the "liberal media"
and academia. In the Occupy movement he saw the seeds of a reversal of this
trend for "cultural populism" to displace "economic populism as a political
force in American life." "Mobs rarely have good answers to problems,"
Meacham said, "and there is no doubt much to be skeptical about in the
crowds making all the noise. But the noise they're making deserves a place
in the broad arena of contending forces."

In the history of modern capitalism, crises are the norm, not the exception.

90

NOURIEL ROUBINI / STEPHEN MIHM

b. 1958 / b. 1968

SOURCE: *Crisis Economics: A Crash Course in the Future of Finance*
DATE: 2011
FIELD: Economic crises

Nouriel Roubini is a prominent American economist who won lasting fame when it emerged he had been one of the few figures to predict the economic crisis that began in 2007. A year earlier he had written a paper for the International Monetary Fund in which he said that the USA faced a housing bust, declining consumer confidence, and recession—a warning which earned him the nickname Dr. Doom.

In 2011 Roubini collaborated with Stephen Mihm, a history professor and writer, on a book that sought to trace the origins of the crisis and to develop a suitable response to future crises. After all, they argued, crises are not anomalies of the modern capitalist system but a normal part of the economic cycle. This was not, they said, a freak occurrence, as much of the financial sector would have you believe, but an inevitable and predictable phenomenon.

While acknowledging that no two crises are identical, the authors plotted their shared characteristics—typically, a combination of easy credit, financial deregulation, an irrational "bubble" (in the case of 2007, housing) and then the inevitable economic collapse. Moreover, the authors argued, where moral hazard thrives in a "too big to fail" culture (see page 139) and the financial sector incentivizes its workers to take huge risks for short-term profits, regulation is vital—from breaking up mega-institutions and separating out high-risk ventures from utility functions, to reining back banker bonuses and confronting bubbles using monetary policy.

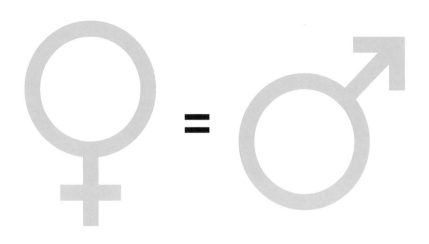

Gender equality and women's empowerment bring huge economic benefits.

91

MICHELLE BACHELET

MICHELLE BACHELET
b. 1951

SOURCE: *Huffington Post*
DATE: 2012
FIELD: Feminist economics

Bachelet—a medical doctor by training—has unimpeachable credentials as a champion of women's rights. She was the first woman to serve as Chile's minister of defense and its first female president (serving from 2006 to 2010 and again from 2014 to 2018), bookending a stint as the executive director of the United Nations Entity for Gender Equality and the Empowerment of Women—commonly known as UN Women.

In this latter role, Bachelet not only fought for greater rights and opportunities for women but made a powerful case that gender equality is good for the wider economy. As she told the *Huffington Post*: "One of the factors a country's economy depends on is human capital. If you don't provide women with adequate access to healthcare, education and employment, you lose at least half of your potential. So, gender equality and women's empowerment bring huge economic benefits."

Bachelet has also highlighted the findings of the World Economic Forum's 2010 global gender gap report, which indicated that the countries with the highest standards of gender equality generally have faster-growing, more competitive economies. Referring to the UN Food and Agriculture Organization's analysis of global farming, Bachelet also suggested that with more than 50 percent of farmers in the developing world being women, by increasing their access to resources such as credit, water, and technological support, food production could be increased by 4 percent—reducing the number of those going hungry by over 100 million. "Gender equality," she insists, "is the right thing to do, but it's also a smart thing to do."

Over time, the welfare state has become [...] a victim of its own success.

92

NIALL FERGUSON

b. 1964

SOURCE: CNN
DATE: 2012
FIELD: Welfare economics

When asked why he believed the West is in decline, Ferguson—a British historian and social commentator—pointed to two main causes. Firstly, emerging economies such as China and India have adopted Western modes of economic dynamism to drive their own expansion. Secondly, the West itself has lost that sense of dynamism. This is down in part, Ferguson suggests, to rising levels of debt among developed nations as a result of high public spending. This debt, he says, represents a "tax on the future" and a "breach of contract between the current generation and the next generations." Where the West was once predicated on principles of self-sacrifice in the interests of the future, the culture has changed to one that champions living in the moment, he argues.

In particular, Ferguson cites the significant expansion of welfare provision since the Second World War. He contends that although initially successful in reducing inequality by transferring resources from rich to poor, the welfare state has become dysfunctional as a result of this success. "It became so successful at prolonging life," he says, "that it becomes financially unsustainable, unless you make major changes to things like retirement ages. And everywhere you see the same basic story, whether you're looking at northern Europe, southern Europe, or North America—welfare states become harder and harder to finance, and structural budget deficits emerge."

Even in periods of economic health, Western economies thus find themselves burdened by deficits, whereas the most dynamic emerging economies of the East generally do not offer their citizens equivalent welfare provision.

The black family survived
centuries of slavery and
generations of Jim Crow,
but it has disintegrated in the
wake of the liberals' expansion
of the welfare state.

93

b. 1930

SOURCE: "Liberalism Versus Blacks" on creators.com
DATE: 2013
FIELD: Welfare economics

Sowell, a senior fellow at the Hoover Institution of Stanford University, has made a name for himself by questioning the efficacy of modern liberal thinking. He has written several books on the subject of the black experience, routinely arguing that progress is less related to progressive governmental policies than is generally credited. As such, he has become a poster boy for advocates of laissez-faire classical liberalism, libertarians, and conservatives. As he put it in 2013: "There is no question that liberals do an impressive job of expressing concern for blacks. But do the intentions expressed in their words match the actual consequences of their deeds?"

Sowell cites the case of San Francisco, a city "unexcelled in its liberalism" but which nonetheless boasts a black population half what it was in 1970, despite the overall population growing over that time. The reason, he suggests, is that restrictions on home building have elevated house prices and rents to a level that saw many blacks on moderate incomes driven out. He goes on to attack the raising of the minimum wage as misguided, since, he contends, it causes spikes in unemployment among the country's low-paid black workers.

As the quote opposite suggests, he is equally scathing of the welfare state, which he believes has contributed to the disintegration of black families. While 22 percent of black children were raised by only one parent in 1960, the figure had risen to 67 percent in 1985—the welfare safety net encouraging family splits. Liberals, he argues, assume positions that make them look good and feel good but show little interest in the actual consequences of those policies.

No hypocrisy is
too great when economic
and financial elites are
obliged to defend
their interest.

94

THOMAS PIKETTY
b. 1971

SOURCE: *Capital in the Twenty-First Century*
DATE: 2014
FIELD: Inequality

Thomas Piketty, a French economist, saw his book, *Capital in the Twenty-First Century*, top bestseller charts amid a blaze of controversy. To his fans, he poses a much-needed challenge to the economic elites whose wealth blocks social mobility, while his critics portray him as a sort of crazed pseudo-Marxist. Central to Piketty's thesis is the notion that modern capitalism enshrines inequality, since wherever the rate of return on capital outstrips the rate of growth (as is often the case), inherited wealth grows faster than earned wealth.

This concentration of "old money" is incompatible, Piketty says, with popularly held notions of democracy and social justice. Backed by evidence of rising inequality since the latter part of the 20th century, Piketty's conclusions run contrary to the orthodoxy encapsulated in the Kuznets curve (see page 145), which suggests industrialized nations enjoy decreasing levels of inequality over time.

So how might this problem be addressed? Among Piketty's most striking suggestions is to punitively tax inherited wealth and raise rates for high earners. The moral justification for capitalism, he suggests, is redundant, if we return to an Austenesque world where it makes more sense to marry into wealth than it does to seek it through hard work, ingenuity, and entrepreneurship. That the mid-20th century enjoyed sustained and growing equality was, he concludes, a blip caused by a cocktail of historical factors, including war, the labor movement, demographics, and technical innovation. A repeat, he says, is unlikely, given the overriding power of capital, but a new system of progressive taxation represents our best hope of turning the tide.

Migration presents policy challenges—but also represents an opportunity to enhance human development, promote decent work, and strengthen collaboration.

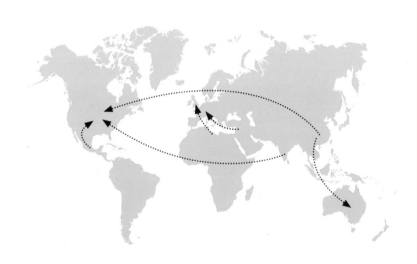

95

BAN KI-MOON
b. 1944

SOURCE: Remarks at opening of the Fourth EU–Africa Summit
DATE: 2014
FIELD: Migration

A South Korean diplomat, Ban Ki-Moon served as Secretary-General of the United Nations from 2007 to 2016. His term was marked by severe migration crises, particularly from war-ravaged areas such as Syria into Europe. The number of international migrants globally rose from 175 million in 2000 to 244 million in 2015, with inevitable points of stress exacerbated by the afteraffects of the global economic crisis of the late 2000s. With developed nations attempting to reboot their diminished economies, the influx of migrants both in search of asylum and work has led to widespread social tensions. Nonetheless, Ban's optimistic view of the benefits and opportunities presented by migration are rooted in hard data.

In 2014 the Organization for Economic Co-operation and Development (OECD)—an intergovernmental economic organization charged with stimulating economic progress and world trade—released a report entitled "Is migration good for the economy?" It related that migrants accounted for almost half of the increase in the American workforce over the previous decade, and 70 percent in Europe. Moreover, migrants filled important roles both in fast-growing and declining sectors of the economy, contributing to increased labor-market flexibility. It also went some way to dispelling the myth that migrants typically represent a net drain on the public purse. Rather, the report stated, migrants contribute more in taxes and social contributions than they receive in benefits. Many also arrive with skills that contribute to the overall development of the receiving nation's human capital by spurring research, innovation, and economic growth. In the boldest terms, where migration expands the workforce, aggregate GDP typically grows.

We're now in the seventh year of a slump brought on by Wall Street excess.

96

b. 1953

SOURCE: "Iron Men of Wall Street" in the *New York Times*
DATE: 2014
FIELD: Financial services

The 2008 Economics Nobel Prize-winner Paul Krugman considers himself on the liberal wing of the political and economic spectrum. The economic crisis that began in 2007 only served to fuel his suspicion that the US's economic elite—especially the financial institutions that dominate Wall Street—had driven the economy into the ground for their own gain.

Writing in 2014, Krugman identified the upper tiers of income distribution as being dominated by executives from the corporate, finance, real estate, and legal sectors. The long-running downturn, he argued, was thanks to "Wall Street excess." "The wizardly job of 'allocating the economy's investment resources,'" he said, "consisted, we now know, largely of funneling money into a real estate bubble, using fancy financial engineering to create the illusion of sound, safe investment." In other words, the banks used other people's money to fund a housing credit boom that was sustainable if nothing ever went wrong. But something, inevitably, did go wrong, forcing individuals and countries around the world to slash their spending to pay down debt.

Writing for the *New York Times* in 2011, Krugman had identified the underlying problem as "more than two decades of growing complacency in wealthy nations, a complacency whose main financial manifestation was ever-growing leverage." "Anyway," he concludes, "the wolves of Wall Street are more Gordon Gekko [the fictional antihero of the movie *Wall Street* who lived by the credo "Greed is good"] than Iron Man [Marvel Comics' business magnate-turned-superhero]; if they're the best argument you have for the justice of extreme inequality, you're not doing too well."

For too many, the dream of economic mobility has been replaced with a nightmare of economic stagnation.

97

ANDREW CUOMO
b. 1957

SOURCE: Inauguration address
DATE: 2015
FIELD: Stagnation

Andrew Cuomo, who trained as a lawyer, became the Democratic governor of New York in 2011—a role his father, Mario Cuomo, had held for three terms in the 1980s and 1990s. As he embarked on his own second term, Cuomo Jr. was well aware of the plight of the poor, having served as chair of the New York City Homeless Commission from 1990 to 1993. "We work harder and we earn less," he told his audience in 2015. "Income inequality is at the highest point in over a century. While American capitalism never guaranteed success, it did guarantee opportunity." But now, he said, the specter of economic stagnation had overwhelmed the hope of economic mobility.

That the US economy (along with many others throughout the world) stagnated post-2007 is evident, although there is much debate as to whether that stagnation is of the cyclical, short-term type or is so-called "secular stagnation"—a long-term drag on economic development caused by fundamental shifts in the economic landscape. Those who advocate the secular stagnation argument point to a number of causes. Some cite long-term insufficient investment in education and infrastructure, while others suggest that the digital revolution has been less capital-dependent than previous "industrial revolutions," meaning lower demand for the sort of investment that fuels economic expansion.

Others, like Cuomo, instead see rising inequality as the chief problem—those with the most money tend toward saving a greater proportion of their wealth, while those struggling to make ends meet can't afford to spend at the levels necessary to spur significant growth.

Africa needs to see itself as the leader of the Fourth Industrial Revolution.

98

NANCY KACUNGIRA
b. 1986

SOURCE: Address to World Economic Forum Africa
DATE: 2016
FIELD: Development

An award-winning journalist for organizations including the BBC and an entrepreneur in her own right, Nancu Kacungira is regarded as an expert on African affairs. In 2016 she spoke at a conference in Kigali, Rwanda, for the World Economic Forum in Africa on the theme of "Connecting Africa's Resources through Digital Transformation." The event sought to explore how the digital economy might act as a catalyst for structural transformations and increased prosperity across the continent—especially given the World Economic Forum's suggestion that "Africa's positive economic outlook is under pressure—mainly due to adverse changes in the global economy." It was against this backdrop that Kacungira suggested Africa must take up the mantle of spearheading "the Fourth Industrial Revolution."

Where the First Industrial Revolution relied on steam to power mechanization, the Second on electricity to power mass production, and the Third on information technology and electronics to increase automation, the Fourth Industrial Revolution is expected to exploit a fusion of technologies across the physical, cyber, and biological spheres—as characterized by the "Internet of everything." In many respects, Africa is well placed to take advantage of these cutting-edge developments. It is expected to overtake both India and China in the next quarter-century in terms of working-age population, reaching the billion mark. Moreover, there are already some 200 innovation hubs across the continent and thousands of high-tech related ventures benefiting from significant banks of venture capital. If the continent is able to embrace Kacungira's aspiration, Africa's prospects are indeed bright.

There's a

big

industry around Bitcoin.

99

RICHARD BRANSON

b. 1950

SOURCE: Interview with Bloomberg News
DATE: 2016
FIELD: Cryptocurrencies

Richard Branson, the billionaire founder of the Virgin Group that controls some 400 companies, spoke these words in response to a question about the fast-emerging phenomenon of cryptocurrency, of which Bitcoin is the largest. In Branson's opinion, it could herald an "economic revolution." So, what is a cryptocurrency? In short, it is a payment system conducted on digital platforms free—unlike traditional currencies—of interference from third parties such as central banks. All transactions are conducted directly peer-to-peer, verified using encryption techniques, and logged in a public ledger known as a blockchain.

Bitcoin itself emerged in 2009, the creation of a shadowy software developer whose identity has never been conclusively established. Advocates of cryptocurrencies point out various advantages over traditional money. For one thing, all transactions are discreet and untraceable—including by state revenue-collecting agencies. Nor are there any banks or regulators to interfere in the flow of payments.

Critics, on the other hand, suggest that such secrecy renders Bitcoin a natural tool for criminal organizations. The rapidly escalating value of Bitcoin (from less than a cent per unit in 2010 to almost $20,000 in 2017) has led to fears of a commodity bubble. In 2014, investor Warren Buffett (see page 147) urged: "Stay away from it. It's a mirage, basically." Yet others remain hopeful of its potential. As Branson put it: "Well, I think it is working [...] People have made fortunes off Bitcoin; some have lost money. It is volatile, but people make money off of volatility too."

The effect of
the concentration
of wealth is to yield
concentration
of power.

100

NOAM CHOMSKY
b. 1928

SOURCE: *Requiem for the American Dream*
DATE: 2017
FIELD: Inequality

Noam Chomsky is a famed American linguist, philosopher, and activist. Associated with the New Left in the 1960s and 1970s, he has been a vocal critic of US foreign policy and neoliberal philosophies of unregulated, laissez-faire economics. *Requiem for the American Dream* was the book he wrote based on a documentary released the previous year in which he argued that rising economic inequality had a "corrosive, harmful effect on democracy" by concentrating power in the hands of the rich few. This path began with the rapid concentration of wealth in the 1970s, Chomsky asserts, when plutocratic interests began to take over. The result, he suggests, has been an assault on lower- and middle-class people, accelerated by the rise of neoliberalism and what he regards as the excessive influence of financial institutions and elites in shaping public life.

The ideal of the "American Dream"—that you might be born poor, work hard, and get rich—has been fundamentally undermined, Chomsky suggests. Whereas in the 1940s and 1950s the average American worker could anticipate owning a home and a car and living a life of relative comfort, that trajectory of upward class mobility is becoming an aspiration for a diminishing number as levels of personal debt rise significantly for the younger generations. It is, he says, "a result of over 30 years of a shift in social and economic policy, completely against the will of the population." "There's nothing surprising about this," he goes on. "That's what happens when you put power in the hands of a narrow sector."

INDEX

CREDITS

SHUTTERSTOCK

8 © Kong_niti 10 © MidoSemsem 16 © Morphart Creation 24 © Morphart Creation 26 © Lynea 30 © Morphart Creation 38 © mikecphoto 42 © Slonomysh; © Morphart Creation 46 © Hein Nouwens 48 © Everett Historical 50 © Gearstd 52 © MaraZe 60 © Shutterstock 68 © Zbynek Jirousek 72 © Everett Historical 98 © bitt24 104 © GeniusKp 112 © Hung Chung Chih 136 © Everett Historical 138 © pterwort 142 © emkaplin 152 © Bart Sadowski 164 © Thomas Yeoh 166 © David Fowler 174 © Antonio Scorza 192 © Evan El-Amin 196 © photo.ua 198 © alisafarov 202 © AnnaGarmatiy 204 © deepspace

ALAMY

6 © Lou-Foto / Alamy Stock Photo 18 © Alamy Stock Photo 34 © Heritage Image Partnership Ltd / Alamy Stock Photo 40 © IanDagnall Computing / Alamy Stock Photo 70 © Art Library / Alamy Stock Photo 80 © GL Archive / Alamy Stock Photo 92 © Alamy Stock Photo 122 © Alamy Stock Photo

US LIBRARY OF CONGRESS
28 © LOC 74 © LOC

Unless listed here, all images are in the public domain.